A *WESTERN HORSEMAN* BOOK

LEGENDARY RANCHES

D1573286

The Horses, History and Traditions of
North America's Great Contemporary Ranches

Contributors
Holly Endersby, Guy de Galard,
Kathy McCraine and Tim O'Byrne

Edited by
Fran Devereux Smith and Cathy Martindale

Photography by
John Brasseaux, Guy de Galard, Ross Hecox,
Ursula Lewis, Kathy McCraine and Tim O'Byrne

Legendary Ranches

Published by
WESTERN HORSEMAN° magazine
3850 North Nevada Ave.
Box 7980
Colorado Springs, Colorado 80933-7980
800-877-5278

www.westernhorseman.com

Design, Typography, and Production
Western Horseman
Fort Worth, Texas

Front Cover Photo By
Lisa Norman
Back Cover Photo By
John Brasseaux

Printing
Branch Smith
Fort Worth, Texas

Manufactured in the United States of America

First Printing: November 2007

ISBN 978-0911647-80-8

INTRODUCTION

Welcome to *Legendary Ranches,* the newest addition to our *Western Horseman* line of books.

What defines a legendary ranch? A few words in the book subtitle, *The Horses, History and Traditions* of *North America's Great Contemporary Ranches,* create a fairly clear picture.

Horses, of course, are involved; after all, horses play the major role on traditional ranching outfits, just as they do here at *Western Horseman.* As for history, these ranches have carved out their places through time, and we can honor their efforts because we've spent almost three-quarters of a century doing the same thing. With time comes tradition, no matter the brand someone rides for, and each outfit forms its unique habits and methods in the workplace. Yet when a historic, tradition-bound outfit—even one that still works horseback—survives, it's typically heralded as a contemporary success for embracing unusual ideas and innovative techniques to move forward in the modern world.

And that's a legendary ranch in a nutshell— one that honors the past with its horseback traditions, but withstands time's test by continually stepping toward the future.

An Easy Evolution

The idea of adding a volume about outstanding ranches to our *Western Horseman* Legends Series developed in a natural way, an easy evolution fostered by both our readers and our staff.

As often is the case with publications such as ours, readers let us know their preferences about the materials we publish. Whenever a *Western Horseman* writer, photographer or advertising representative travels cross-country, he or she often returns home with feedback to share. Ranching in the West, we've learned, is a favorite subject among our readers. They not only share their thoughts on our ranching coverage, but also information about possible sources for such articles.

As a result, when our previous book editor polled *Western Horseman* staffers, asking about ranches worthy of inclusion in a book she envisioned about legendary outfits, few of us were at a loss for names. We dug through our "possibles" files for supporting data and contact information for ranches. And the book editor's list quickly grew.

In fact, the list grew exponentially to include far more ranches than one book could contain. So if your favorite ranch isn't included within this book, stay tuned; a second such volume is a distinct possibility.

However, for this volume a few parameters were set that primarily relate to ranches in terms of those four important words—horses, history, traditions and the contemporary. The ranches included here have vibrant histories, continue to use horses in traditional cowboy ways and currently remain successful operations. Size, climate and terrain aren't everything, but such considerations certainly can increase the difficulty factor for any horse and cattle outfit trying to remain a viable business enterprise nowadays.

More than anything, perhaps, each chapter provides a snapshot of North American ranching at the turn of the 21st century. Four authors have chronicled the often daring and sometimes flamboyant characters, hard-working ranch horses and, at times, unusual situations that have contributed to each ranch's subsequent success. Because our readers are horse owners and breeders, *Legendary Ranches* focuses on equine bloodlines, routine ranch-horse and cowboy life, and the somewhat recent competitive opportunities that now allow a working ranch cowboy to showcase his equine partner's talents.

Delivering the Goods

As promised in the subtitle, *Legendary Ranches* delivers *"The Horses, History and Traditions of North America's Great Contemporary Ranches,"* all courtesy of four talented writers. Through the years Holly Endersby, Guy de Galard, Kathy McCraine and Tim O'Byrne have contributed numerous feature articles to *Western Horseman* magazine, as well as material for this and other books.

These four authors bring a wealth of ranching and riding experience to their work, as well as strong writing and photography skills. Ranching, of course, is never an easy

proposition, and each author's work reflects both good and bad aspects inherent in the lifestyle. The writing, for example, might tell of devastating blizzards, and the photographs often portray breathtaking scenery.

In addition to these professionals, long-time equine-industry shootist John Brasseaux and *Western Horseman* magazine photographer and senior editor Ross Hecox have focused their cameras on these legendary ranching outfits. They're just two of many, including our Fort Worth production staff and Amarillo, Texas, copy editor, who have made this book possible.

We hope you enjoy everyone's efforts as you read *Legendary Ranches*. Each chapter, it seems, contributes a bit more to the wild, western dreams shared by those of us who love the West and a ranching lifestyle.

Best regards,
Fran Smith
Book Publishing Director

CONTENTS

"To work a crew of good cowboys who really knew what they were doing, to run good cattle, and to ride good horses was just about as close to heaven as a man could get."
Bill Howell

1

BABBITT RANCHES

By Kathy McCraine

On the Cataract Plains north of Williams, Ariz., the March wind howled across the Coconino Plateau like a stampeding herd. The sea of yellow grass, whipped to a frenzy, stretched endlessly to the horizon, rimmed by low azure mesas, while storm clouds swirled above, as yet undecided what the day would bring. The lonely gravel road, snaking for miles across the plain, seemed eons away from busy Highway 64, where carloads of tourists sped northward to the Grand Canyon. Here and there in the distance, Hereford cattle dotted the landscape like tiny red ants on a yellow canvas.

Vic Howell, manager of the historic Babbitt Ranches, had assembled his cowboy crew to gather and work some 2,200

Babbitt Ranches received the 2005 Best Remuda Award from the American Quarter Horse Association and Bayer Animal Health.

7

Now retired, Bill Howell, as manager, wielded enormous influence on the Babbitt Ranches' horse program.

The Start of an Empire

In the mid-1880s, exciting stories of undeveloped land and investment opportunities sparked the Babbitt Brothers' imaginations. In February 1886, David and Billy Babbitt left their Cincinnati, Ohio, home with $20,000 in savings and journeyed west intending to purchase a New Mexico cattle ranch. On arrival, they learned that land prices there had risen prohibitively, but a railroad clerk told them of virtually undiscovered lush grazing land near Flagstaff in the Arizona Territory.

At Flagstaff the brothers found the promised grassland, but there could have been little to impress them about the town. The newcomers stepped off the train to find a few ramshackle buildings and canvas tents, erected after a fire had leveled the business district. Less determined men would have walked away, but the Babbitts were no ordinary men. They took the gamble that would eventually pay off in an empire. Within a month they had begun to purchase land and had a herd of cattle trailed out from Kansas. In honor of their hometown, Cincinnati, Ohio, the Babbitts adopted the "CO Bar" as their brand.

The railroad's arrival in northern Arizona in the early 1880s had aided a booming cattle business by opening eastern markets. Land was cheap, and cattle prices skyrocketed. Their future must have indeed looked bright to the enterprising Babbitt Brothers. But disaster struck when the great blizzards of 1886 and '87 wiped out millions of cattle in the West. Prices plummeted, and in its first year of operation, the CO Bar was nearly wiped out.

For the next 30 years droughts and bad markets plagued the Babbitts' operations, but the brothers persevered and continued to expand. In the early 1900s they added the A-1, or Arizona Cattle Company, followed by the Circle S and the giant Aztec Land & Cattle Company, also known as the Hashknife, due to its brand, which was shaped like the hand-forged hash knife bunkhouse cooks used to prepare the beef dish.

Texas cattleman John N. Simpson first registered the brand in 1874 when he established a ranch west of Fort Worth, according to historian Jim Bob Tinsley in his book, *The Hash Knife Brand*. Cattle from the extensive holdings that Simpson and his partners amassed eventually were purchased to stock the Aztec Land & Cattle Company, a 2 million-acre

yearling calves running on the ranch's west side, known as the Cataract. Bundled in heavy coats, the cowboys rode hunched against the wind, the older and wiser men having traded their Stetsons and Resistols for wool caps and earmuffs, while young, reckless cowboys clung to tradition, screwing their felts down tightly.

Little by little, small bunches of cattle, each flanked by a single rider, converged on Blanco Tank until a massive herd formed and began to move slowly across the flats. It was a breathtaking sight, this marching formation of perfectly matched, bloomy, white-faced Hereford calves. They obviously had wintered well.

This seasonal ritual has been repeated now for 120 years on Arizona's largest privately owned, working cattle ranch. How the Babbitt brothers put together this virtual ranching empire—and even more remarkably, held it together for more than a century—is one of the more fascinating tales of the American West.

Ranch horses are unsaddled during the noon meal, which provides a nice break for the cowboys, too.

ranch established in Arizona in 1884 and later purchased by the Babbitt Brothers.

By 1919 the Babbitts owned or operated almost every ranch in northern Arizona from Ash Fork, west of Flagstaff, to the New Mexico border. They ran thousands of cattle and sheep on 100,000 square miles of range, some 3 million acres in Arizona, California and Kansas. The brothers also owned a multitude of other businesses, from trading posts to an opera house. Eventually five brothers became involved, with George, David and Edward running the Babbitt Brothers Trading Company, and C.J. and Billy primarily running the ranches.

Consolidating Ranch Operations

The era between World War I and World War II brought more hard times and a depressed cattle market. During this period many Babbitt properties were liquidated. When one of C.J.'s sons, John, became director of ranches in 1939, a period of reorganization followed. He later purchased the Espee Ranch in the 1950s and consolidated the ranch operation into four principal holdings—the CO Bar, Cataract, Hart Ranch (later sold) and the Espee.

John Babbitt was a man of integrity and committed to the ranch, liked and respected by almost everyone who ever knew him or worked for him. Not the least of his admir-

Billy Cordasco, John Babbitt's grandson, has worked in various company operations since age 14, and the old safe has been around even longer.

ers is grandson Billy Cordasco, who, at the young age of 28, took over the company reins in 1991. Billy, raised by his grandparents after his parents' deaths, has worked in various company operations since age 14.

Sitting in the same two-story office building that Babbitts have occupied in downtown Flagstaff since 1889, Billy exudes the energy and enthusiasm that must have driven his ancestors before him. Casually dressed in jeans and boots, relaxed in the comfortable clutter of books, vintage ranch photographs and maps, Billy's youthfulness belies the enormous job of presiding over 200 Babbitt shareholders and their families. He is not one to take things for granted or live in the past.

"Babbitts is still here today because we have a philosophy," he said. "We have a land ethic, and we are constantly learning, constantly trying to understand. We have to be ahead of the curve today, as far as understanding ecological issues with the land."

To that end Billy has been instrumental in the company donating large conservation easements to the Nature Conservancy, Coconino County and other entities, as well as in the ranch's participation in holistic range management and watershed assessment projects. Just as his grandfather did, Billy is quick to give credit to the ranch employees, many raised on the ranch, who have remained there to work as adults.

"This has been a tight-knit group of people," he said. "We have an employee base that's very loyal, that feels as much ownership in the ranch as the actual owners."

One example of that loyalty and longevity was Frank Banks, who went to work for CO Bar in 1925. By 1944, he was running the entire operation, and his influence is still felt today. He is credited with establishing the modern ranch operation, initiating the yearling steer and heifer program and designing the intricate watering system that is the outfit's lifeblood, among other innovations.

When Banks retired in 1969, Bill Howell, whose entire family has figured prominently in modern Babbitt Ranches history, filled Banks' position. Today four generations of Howells live and work on the ranch, and Bill is still a "fixture," helping out whenever there is cow work to be done. Tall and lanky, weathered by many long days in the sun, he still sits a horse and drags calves with the best of them.

Harvey Howell first came to the ranch in 1966 and has worked steadily for the outfit since 1979.

Vic Howell became manager of the 700,000-acre ranching operation in 1991.

The Babbitt Ranches Colt Sale, held annually in mid-July, draws buyers nationwide, who pick up their weaned colts the following March.

Clay Rodgers grew up on Babbitt Ranches, where his father began working in 1982.

The Howell Legacy

On October 12, 1963, Bill Howell pulled into Flagstaff with a wife and two babies. The 29-year-old cowboy had driven all night from Utah, headed for the Boquillas Ranch at Seligman, Ariz., where he hoped to find a desperately needed job.

"I went downtown that day to buy a pair of oxbow stirrups," he recalled, "and everywhere I looked, I saw Babbitt, Babbitt, Babbitt. I had heard of the Babbitt Ranches, and by the time I made the circle and got to Babbitt Ford, I thought, 'Well, I might just go to work for them instead.'"

At the Ford dealership, Bill got the phone number of the man doing the ranch hiring— Frank Banks. When he called, Banks' wife told him the wagon was out, but he was welcome to drive out and look for her husband. When Bill stopped for directions, she asked if he would take a couple of clean shirts to her husband. Those two shirts would change Bill's life forever.

He found Frank Banks that day, a tall, pencil-thin man who stood about 6 feet, 5 inches. "I introduced myself and told him I was looking for a job," Bill recalled. "He said, 'Well, I've got a full crew.' So I thanked him and went back to my pickup."

Just then Bill remembered the clean shirts in a paper sack on his truck seat, and he walked back to the corral, where Frank was unsaddling his horse. As an afterthought, Frank said, "We're camped over here about five miles, and you can eat lunch with us if you've got time."

Time was one thing Bill had, so he agreed "Sure."

Frank must have had time to think about things, because at lunch he asked Bill, "Are you a rough-stock rider?"

When Bill replied in the affirmative, Frank said, "I have some spoiled horses, and if you want a job, I'll give them to you to ride."

Bill took the job, and thus began the 28-year career that would make him one of the best known and most widely respected cattlemen in Arizona. Bill stayed with the wagon at the Cataract that fall, drawing $250 a month, which included a $50 premium for riding the spoiled horses, pretty good cowboy wages in those days.

Then Frank began moving Bill around to different camps, and after one year asked if Bill was planning to stay on. "What I've got in mind is that I'd like to see you have my job someday," Frank told Bill.

Two years later, in 1967, Frank moved Bill to the CO Bar. He remembers it as one of the most frustrating times of his career. "We moved to the COs in the spring of 1967. They had lots of cattle. I didn't know the country, and my crew supposedly did, and they were all upset with me being named the boss."

To add to Bill's difficulties, that was the year of the big snowstorm, a winter no Arizona cattleman or cowboy will ever forget.

"It was about December 13, and we were working late that fall," Bill recalled, "weaning calves at Spider Web. We had about 500 cows shut in the water lot, and we were going to trail them to a place called Canyon Storage the next morning. That morning it was snowing like a son-of-a-gun. That mesa country at

Through the years, the Babbitts, as the ranch is known, has hired a lot of Texas cowboys on the wagon.

Spider Web is a big piece of country, flat with no trees and no real landmarks. I looked at that a little bit and said, 'Boys, I don't know that I can find Canyon Storage in this storm.' So we loaded our horses and went back to the house."

It continued to snow, so the next morning the cowboys opened the gate and let the cows go with the storm. They drifted all the way to the Little Colorado River, and the snow continued day after day. On the 10th day, it cleared enough to begin plowing trails with a Caterpillar so cattle could get to water. With 36 inches of snow, it was a slow process.

"We were horseback from daylight to dark every day," Bill said, "and it was a cold son-of-a-gun, about zero degrees. We had 1,700 weaner calves in a pasture, scattered out in twos and threes. If we roped one and dragged it through the snow, we could get the others to follow to the cat track.

"Cattle had just given up, and would stand out there. We didn't get to some of the cows for 30 days, and it was surprising how they were still alive. I guess they didn't burn any energy, and they didn't need much water because they didn't eat anything."

Ultimately, the ranch suffered about a 5 percent death loss from the storm. Bill eventually became known as a tough manager, who expected as much from his men as he did from himself.

"I was a hardworking man, who pretty much walked my own path," he said. "I expected my men to be to work on time, and if a man didn't show up, I fired him. And I expected every camp man to ride his country and to have a project to improve his camp. On the other hand, I was always the type of person who told a man what I wanted done, and then left him alone. A lot of times there are two ways to go around the hill; it's the results that I was interested in."

The Ranch Today

In 1991 Bill Howell retired, and the manager position passed to his son, Victor, who still has a shy, boyish grin despite the gray sprinkling his hair. As did Billy Cordasco, Vic graduated from Northern Arizona University

Scott Westlake sorts the mares and foals prior to the annual colt sale.

with a business degree and, as with Billy, Vic was a young 29 to shoulder such a huge responsibility. Much like his dad, Vic has gone on to establish himself as a competent and well-respected cattleman.

The ranching operation today totals 700,000 acres, running all the way from Interstate 40 to the Grand Canyon. The 275-section Cataract and 225-section Espee ranches join one another to form one large, square chunk of land on the west side of Highway 64. The 640-section CO Bar runs from the Little Colorado River, which borders the Navajo reservation, to the Grand Canyon, then west, just 10 miles short of Highway 64. The CO Bar begins on the rolling volcanic plains shadowed by the imposing San Francisco Peaks and ends up in the tall pines and aspens, where three summer U.S. Forest Service permits are located. The Cataract and Espee are mainly plains, mostly grama grassland with some scattered cedar trees. Ranch elevations range from 4,500 feet on the Little Colorado River to 8,500 feet at the highest point.

The CO Bar runs 2,400 mother cows, and the Cataract 1,500 mother cows. All the weaned calves to be shipped, around 3,000 in a decent year, are held over and run on the Espee, then sold as yearlings in the fall. On the CO Bar, heifers are marked with that brand, while the W Triangle brand is used on the Cataract. Both ranches use the Bar V Bar on all the steers. Horses are branded with the Hashknife on the left hip.

The CO Bar has a number of summer and winter camps, including the main headquarters at Spider Web Camp, north of Flagstaff, where Vic and his wife, Jamie, and two other families live. The Espee and Cataract each has two camps, with families living at three of the four camps, and one just a winter camp for single men.

Working Cattle

Cattle work today at Babbitt Ranches is little different than it was 120 years ago, except that, with good roads throughout the rolling country, goosenecks and a bobtail truck are used to haul horses sometimes as

Catching a horse from the remuda remains part of the daily ranch routine.

far away as 12 miles. Horses are taught to jump three or four feet from flat ground right into the bed of the bobtail truck, known to the hands as the "little rack."

Vic likes to have a crew of 10 to 12 cowboys for branding in the spring and gathering in the fall, which means hiring about four extra men, many of them young cowboys who come from as far away as Texas and Wyoming. The men stay at the various camps, rolling out their bedrolls in the bunkhouse or pitching tepees. The "chuck wagon," which is taken to the camps with the supplies, is actually an old Ford truck made out like a chuck wagon.

"We don't have a 'wagon' per se," Vic explained. "But we say we pull out a spring and fall wagon, and basically that refers to when all the cowboys get together and start the branding or cattle work."

The spring wagon runs from May 1 to June 30, and the fall wagon from Labor Day until Thanksgiving, about three months. Branding pens are located at various ranch water holes,

where cowboys might brand 150 to 300 calves in a morning's time. The biggest weaning takes place at the CO Bar, where close to 1,000 head are weaned at once, due to the way the place is laid out, long and narrow.

"We might gather for three days out of a big pasture into a 30- or 40-section pasture," Vic said, "and then the next morning trail them to the weaning corrals and wean, leaving the calves on one side of the corral and the cows on the other. Then the following morning we'll trail those cows 12 miles to the winter country."

One thing that sets Babbitts apart: It is one of the last remaining big ranches in Arizona to run straight Hereford cattle. When Bill Howell took over as manager, he and John Babbitt discussed how to improve cattle productivity. Impressed with the 26 Bar Herefords from Springerville, Ariz., the men struck a deal to purchase bulls in volume.

Though bulls now come from several sources, Vic doesn't foresee any changes.

Wrangling the remuda midday at the Spider Web Camp usually stirs a cloud of dust.

"We've always said, 'If it's working, why change it?'"

For the past seven years he has marketed the cattle on the Internet through Crossroads Cattle Company, one small concession to modern times.

The Babbitt Horses

As old, 19th-century photographs show, Babbitt Ranches has been breeding good horses from the beginning. As with many big outfits, though, the ranch had little interest in getting registration papers on its horses when the American Quarter Horse Association was formed, so little is known about the early bloodlines. In 1964, when AQHA offered one last chance to register horses before closing the books, the ranch had its mares inspected for registration. Prior to that only the stallions had been registered.

Bill Howell is generally credited with turning around the horse program in the 1960s. "When Bill came, they didn't know which mares were producing the good horses," Vic said, "so he took it on himself to know and remember those horses. Now we're raising some pretty good horses because he kept weeding those bad ones out and keeping the good ones."

These mares and foals are at the Spider Web Camp on the CO Bar.

A short break gives cowboys an opportunity to plan the next move with the cattle and allows the horses time to water.

A ranch
cowboy
pushes the
herd at the
Tin House
Camp.

Most of the horses today go back to Naco, a Greene Cattle Company stallion from Cananea, Mexico, and to Beaver, a horse Frank Banks bought in the 1940s. When Bill Howell started at Babbitts, Clabber Boy, a Clabber-bred horse, had replaced Beaver.

"Those Clabber horses were awfully good, stout horses with a lot of endurance," Bill said, "but they were kind of cranky. They were hard to start, and they were nasty-bucking boogers—that's the reason I went to work riding the rough string. But all that's bred out of them now. You had a different environment back then; you had a lot more cowboys, a lot more work, and the ranch wasn't fenced like it is now."

Some of the quality stallions bought under Bill's management included Ginger Bars Hank, a grandson of Sugar Bars; a Hancock-bred horse named Pocho, by Frosty Joe; and Deck of Wood by Speedy II by Driftwood. Some Doc Bar blood also was infused along the way.

Today the ranch runs about 75 mares and uses six stallions. The broodmare band is heavy on Driftwood breeding, mainly through a 25-percent Driftwood-bred stallion, Cowboy Drift. And a Tonto Bars Hank grandson, Hanks Chargin Bar, has infused a high percentage of King blood.

Two of the newer stallions being out-crossed on the Driftwoods are Proudgun, a son of Playgun, and Ima Bed Of Cash, a Dash For Cash grandson. The ranch also recently leased Red Hot Line, a Red Hot Hancock son with AQHA performance points in heading, heeling and calf roping.

"We're trying to shoot for a rodeo-type horse that will work for heading and heeling or calf roping, but one that also will make a ranch horse," Vic explained. "You need the right mix—a horse with speed to compete in roping, but also the cow and athletic ability of a cutting horse."

Stallions are ridden on the ranch and treated just as if they are geldings when it isn't breeding season. Fillies are started at age 2, and given 10 to 20 rides. If they have what it takes to produce good ranch horses, they are turned in with the mares. The remuda consists of about 80 geldings, with each cowboy having six to seven horses in his mount.

In 2005 Babbitt Ranches received the coveted Best Remuda Award from the AQHA and Bayer Animal Health, which honors working ranches for the cow horses they produce.

Even further testament to the Babbitts' horse quality is the popularity of the annual Babbitt Ranches Colt Sale, held the second Saturday of July each year, and now a tradition.

The idea evolved in the 1970s when Bill Howell began inviting a few people out to watch the midsummer colt branding. The ranch didn't sell colts, but so many people were interested in buying the fillies that the outfit began inviting more people. In 1980 the ranch held its first real sale at Redlands Camp, and today attendance has grown to more than 400 people, who come from nationwide to purchase the Babbitt Ranches' Driftwood-bred horses.

Now the sale is held at Spider Web Camp, and colts are branded the day before the sale. Buyers pay a $250 deposit on their purchases on sale day. The mares and colts are then turned back on pasture until the following March, when the young horses are weaned and halter-broken before being picked up by the buyers.

Family Affairs

In the ranching world, camp men and cowboys drift outfit to outfit, as if they are playing a game of musical chairs, always looking for greener pastures. Why then have so many families found permanent homes at Babbitts?

Although each man or woman has additional personal reasons, any one of them almost always responds with the same simple answer: "This is just a good outfit to work for."

Harvey Howell, Bill's brother, came to the ranch in 1966 and has worked steadily for Babbitts since 1979. He attributes that to the enjoyment of working good cattle, riding good horses, and being able to raise his family where they all can ride and work together. He and his wife, Janet, whose father worked for C.J. Babbitt, started taking their two sons with them horseback when the boys were still small enough to carry on the fronts of the saddles.

A cowboy drives the gathered yearlings from the Blanco Tank.

"You wonder what keeps you here?" Harvey asked. "Okay, you have a family, you're all riding those good horses, and you broke them yourself. So you get married to a ranch that way. It would just devastate you if you had to leave it and leave all those horses behind."

Not that there aren't drawbacks and dangers inherent in the cowboy's job. Harvey recalled a time some years ago when he was almost killed by a falling horse. "It happened before daylight when we were saddling. I got on a horse that bucked. He bucked into some rocks, and when he hit the rocks, he just flipped over. I wound up on the ground facedown. I was just thinking momentarily in my mind, 'I wonder where that horse is.' And about that time the saddle horn hit me right in the middle of the back."

It was a 20-mile gallop to get a pickup and carry Harvey out, because the crew had been trailered far out on the range. It wound up being three hours before they got Harvey to a hospital, where doctors found that his lungs had collapsed, and his ribs and back were broken. Luckily he lived through it all, and in six weeks was back on a horse as if nothing happened. Just another wreck in a cowboy's life.

Tad Dent has worked for Babbitts since 1985, and before him, his dad, Tracy, started wrangling horses there when he was 17. Tad never thought about doing anything but cowboying. To him it's all fun, especially halter-breaking the colts.

"It's just fun messing with those little boogers," he said. "Then you watch them grow up, and you watch them when they're broke, and you know how their minds work. I like working the big herds outside, too, watching those cows and remembering each calf. Some of them stick out, whether it's the markings on them, or the shape of their horns, or just their personalities."

Ranch cowboys typically spend a couple of months each spring branding calves.

The Redlands Camp is known by that name for an obvious reason.

"And riding good horses is fun too. Like that 'Woody' horse I had one time. We were working the herd in the alley, and he jumped plumb across the alley sideways. He pinned a steer against the fence, just mashed him against the fence until the steer bawled and backed up. Now, when you're riding a horse that can jump 12 feet sideways, that's fun."

All three of Vic's daughters wound up marrying Babbitt cowboys, and two of the women are still at the ranch. The oldest, Victoria, was raised riding and working on the ranch. Petite, with long brown hair and her dad's serious eyes, she admits to feeling that the Babbitts is "my family ranch."

There was no question that she would marry a cowboy, but her first impression of Scott Westlake, the tall, slender, Wyoming horseman who would become her husband, was hardly love at first sight. He wore a flat, Wyoming-style hat that was brown, of all things—not the acceptable black or silver belly of an Arizona cowboy.

Vickie once complained to her mother, "There's nobody around here to date, no good guys."

Her mom asked, "What about Scott?"

"Mom," she said, " I could never date a guy with a flat hat!"

Scott thought Vickie was "probably as good a hand at ranch-type cowboy work" as any girl he'd ever been around, "and she handled a rope real good." After he changed his hat style, they were married in 1999 and today live at Redlands Camp with their two girls, Katherine and Rebecca. Katherine, riding a gentle horse, already trails behind her dad.

Another of Vic's daughters, Danielle, is married to Babbitt cowboy Clay Rodgers. Danielle and Clay live at the Espee Camp with their infant son, Tom. Clay grew up on the ranch, and his dad, Jack, has worked there since 1982.

Holding With Tradition

Even with that brand of loyalty from present employees, the biggest cloud on the Babbitt Ranches' horizon and the future's biggest challenge—except, of course, for recurring droughts—is finding the right hands. There is a limited supply of people willing to give up better paying, more comfortable jobs in town for the cowboy life, and the company has no intention of changing anything.

"People ask me, 'Do you think it is still feasible to work cattle horseback?'" Billy Cordasco said with a laugh.

"I ask them, 'Are you going to quit using horses when gas could go to $7 per gallon?'"

He can only hope that cowboys continue to have the same philosophy Bill Howell always has had. Cowboying might not have made him a rich man, but clearly he wouldn't have traded his life for any other.

"I have enjoyed every day that I worked," Bill once said. "I never said, 'Damn, I'm glad that job's over.' I enjoyed punching cows, really enjoyed it. And to work a crew of good cowboys who really knew what they were doing, to run good cattle, and to ride good horses was just about as close to heaven as a man could get."

Babbitt Ranches Timeline

1886: David and Billy Babbitt left Cincinnati, Ohio, to purchase a New Mexico cattle ranch, but, instead, bought land in Arizona. Their brand, the CO Bar, honors their hometown.

1889: The Babbitt brothers opened offices in the same Flagstaff, Ariz., building that houses ranch offices today. The ranching operation survived and expanded to include the A-1 or Arizona Cattle Company, the Circle S and the Aztec Land & Cattle Company, also known as The Hashknife.

1919: By now, the Babbitts owned or operated almost every ranch in northern Arizona and some beyond its borders, controlling some 100,000 square miles of range, or 3 million acres in three states. C.J. and Billy Babbitt ran the ranching operation, and brothers George, David and Edward operated Babbitt Brothers Trading Company.

1925: Frank Banks began working for the CO Bar and ran the entire outfit by 1944.

1939: John, C. J. Babbitt's son, became director of ranches.

1950s: John Babbitt purchased the Espee Ranch, then consolidated the operation into four principal holdings—the CO Bar, Cataract, the Espee and the Hart Ranch, which was later sold.

1964: Babbitt Ranches registered ranch mares with the American Quarter Horse Association before the registry closed its books. Prior to that, only ranch stallions had been registered.

1969: Frank Banks retired from managing Babbitt Ranches, and Bill Howell, his handpicked successor, stepped into the position.

1980: The first Babbitt Ranches Colt Sale was held in July, although people had attended the midsummer colt-branding, a precursor to the sale, for more than 10 years.

1991: Billy Cordasco, John Babbitt's grandson, took over Babbitt Ranches company operations, and Bill Howell's son, Victor, became manager when Bill retired.

2005: Babbitt Ranches received the Best Remuda Award from the American Quarter Horse Association and Bayer Animal Health, a testament to the fine ranch horses the outfit raises.

"It wouldn't be the same if it was easy, I guess. It's a cowboy deal and a horseback deal, and there will always be something that needs doing with a cow."
Wes Foote

2

O RO RANCH

By Kathy McCraine

The O RO Ranch is different. Many a legendary cowboy's horse has left tracks in the shadow of Mount Hope, the imposing peak at the ranch's center. Mount Hope presides like an ancient pyramid over a grassy plain flanked by high mountain ranges and rugged, gaping canyons. Those horse tracks, tracing back to an old Spanish land grant, have been swept away by time. But memories of them live today in a new generation of men, who still spend their lives looking between the horses' ears and following cattle.

At 257,000 acres, the O RO Ranch, north of Prescott, Ariz., is certainly one of the largest, roughest and most remote ranches

This shot reflects life on the ROs today—and as it was a century ago. Makeshift denim bell boots protect the horse in the rocky terrain.

Jane Droppa, who with brother John Irwin owns the ROs, often rides "Spooks," her favorite ranch horse.

in the state. Burro Canyon, a mere jagged line on the map, separates the ranch from its neighbors to the south, but might as well divide two unique worlds. Cowboys still tell tales of the *orejanas*, the wild unbranded cattle that dwell deep in the canyon. Since it is mostly inaccessible, even horseback, whispered legends of those old mossy-backs still live in the imagination.

Partly because much of the ranch is closed to the public by locked gate, an intangible mystique surrounds the outfit. Anyone who has ever lived or worked there feels it.

Life on "the big outfit," as former manager Bob Sharp called it in his 1974 book by the same name, might be more modernized today, but the people there remain a special breed. As he puts it, they are "more independent, carefree, proud and loyal."

The "ROs," as local cow people know the ranch, is still strictly a horseback outfit, and it is one of the few ranches left that runs a wagon, spring and fall—from necessity, not for show. This ranch is no place for a "wanna-be" cowboy. A hand here best be able to live in a tepee five to six months of the year,

shoe his own horses, mount a snorty horse at daylight, and spend a hard day in the saddle, come rain or shine. Such a man, however, belongs to a dying breed.

Baca Float No. 5

The history of what is now the O RO Ranch dates to the early 1800s. Mexico was still a Spanish colony, and the United States had not yet acquired the New Mexico and Arizona territories through the Gadsden Purchase.

In 1821 the Spanish crown favored Don Luis Maria Baca, a Spanish citizen living in northern New Mexico, with the Las Vegas Grant near the present city of Los Alamos, N.M. Don Luis, a rancher in search of better pastures, prepared a formal petition in his name and those of his 17 children. He was granted almost 500,000 acres of choice grassland, and for a time he and his family lived a good life there.

Unfortunately, a roving band of Navajo Indians in the area took an interest in his fine horses. Eventually, they burned Don Luis' outbuildings and drove off his entire herd of horses and mules. The family, in fear for their lives, abandoned their land and fled.

For several years no one in the family attempted to return to the land grant. Meanwhile, Mexico had gained independence from Spain, and a new set of petitioners settled the land, establishing a substantial colony. When the United States government accepted the Gadsden Purchase Treaty in 1854, the federal government agreed to recognize the validity of the Mexican and Spanish land-grant titles. In 1856, heirs of the now-deceased Don Luis attempted to reclaim the original land grant from settlers who had moved onto the property. To protect U.S. citizens who had settled in the area, the government agreed to "float" the heirs' rights to the original grant, and allowed them to select five tracts of 100,000 acres each elsewhere. The fifth tract the heirs chose was north of Prescott, now part of the O RO Ranch and today one of the largest chunks of deeded land in Arizona. Known as Baca Float No. 5, this is the only land in northern Arizona that can be traced to a Spanish or Mexican grant. It makes up approximately 100,000 acres of the ranch.

The heirs lost no time in selling their Arizona grant, and throughout the 19th century's final decades, title to the Baca Float No. 5 was transferred several times. In 1880, Dr. Edward B. Perrin, a wealthy San Francisco land speculator, wound up with the land title. Perrin's son, Lilo, ran the Baca Float until 1936, when the estate sold the grant to the Greene Cattle Company. For the next 37 years the grant was part of a vast cattle empire accumulated in Mexico and the United States by Colonel William Cornell Greene and his descendants.

Greene Cattle Company

Colonel Greene, a flamboyant character and wheeler-dealer, made and lost fortunes throughout his life. He had been a miner, a prosperous citizen of Tombstone, Ariz., a copper magnate and rancher, according to C. L. Sonnichsen's book, *Colonel Greene and the Copper Skyrocket*. By the turn of the century, Greene, with other investors, had formed the huge Cananea Consolidated Copper Company in Cananea, Mexico, in the state of Sonora, just south of the Arizona border.

But Greene was first and foremost a cow man, and with so much lush, unfenced grassland in Sonora, he was eager to make something of it, just as he'd done in his other enterprises. He formed the Cananea Cattle Company in Mexico in 1901 and the Greene Cattle Company north of the border, where he had large land holdings along the San Pedro River in southern Arizona.

Greene registered the "RO" brand in Mexico and the "OR" brand north of the border. Later his cattle in the United States would be branded with an O on the left ribs and an RO on the left hip. The horses were, and still are, branded with an RO on the left hip.

At its height, the Cananea Cattle Company controlled 1 million acres of grassland, including land leased from the copper company. According to a 1983 *Quarter Horse Journal* article, the outfit ran more than 45,000 head of cattle and 3,000 horses.

However, by 1907 Greene was in financial trouble, having overextended his investments in the copper mine, timber mills and railroads. The Anaconda Corporation took over the mine that year. Fortunately, Greene had enough foresight to put all his ranch holdings in the name of his second wife, Mary. When all his other enterprises crashed around him, Greene still had 800,000 acres of ranch land on both sides of the border.

His cattle now became his major concern, but Colonel Greene also was a horseman who took great pride in the quality of his ranch

Company president Wayne Word, longtime manager of the ROs, has both riding and desk jobs at the ranch.

The ROs has long had a reputation for raising hardy, capable ranch horses and maintains 100 to 110 geldings in the remuda.

remuda. One story tells of a cavalry captain who approached Greene about purchasing horses. He told Greene he wanted to buy 250 geldings, and specified that they should stand a certain number of hands high and be of a particular age. Greene is said to have replied, "What color do you need?" He then supplied the horses in the specified color.

However, horses caused Greene's death in 1911; when a team ran away, he was thrown from his buggy. Before he died, Greene entrusted his family and ranches to his second-in-command, Charles Wiswall.

A Quick Study

Though he had never seen a cattle operation until he was grown, Wiswall learned fast, and he continued to run and expand the ranches until his death in 1952. He and Mary Greene, the colonel's widow, were married in 1918, and by the end of the 1920s, Wiswall had put the ranching operation in the black for the first time since the colonel's death.

As had Greene, Wiswall also took an interest in the Cananea horses. However, during the Mexican revolution in the 20th century's second decade, Pancho Villa's army confis-

cated most Cananea stallions. So at the revolution's end, Wiswall set out to rebuild the horse herd. He had heard about the "Steel Dust" horses of Texas, and he initially purchased six stallions; five are believed to be of Peter McCue breeding. These horses would be among the first registered in the American Quarter Horse Association when it was formed in 1940.

Lyman Tenney, son-in-law of the late J. Ernest Browning, who was instrumental in starting the AQHA, remembered how these horses came to be included in the association stud registry's first volume. Browning, a renowned rancher and Quarter Horse breeder from Willcox, Ariz., also was an inspector for the fledgling AQHA when the association was preparing to close its books. Wiswall called Browning into Mexico to inspect mares and stallions for registration, and then told Browning to eliminate all but the cream of the crop. After spending 30 to 40 days inspecting some 900 head of horses, Browning had selected 250 for registration.

Wiswall then told him, "Mr. Browning, we appreciate what you've done, and I want you to go and pick six of those 2-year-old fillies for your own." Those fillies become some of the foundation mares in Browning's own reputable breeding program.

The Bob Sharp Years

In 1935, Robert L. Sharp, who had married Greene's daughter, Beebe, went to work for the Cananea Cattle Company. Sharp had been a horse wrangler on the Mexican border, a mucker in a Mohave Desert gold mine and, finally, a partner in a ranch on the Sonora River. He developed a steadfast loyalty to the cattle company and soon became one of Wiswall's most trusted employees.

By 1936, Charlie Wiswall had seen the handwriting on the wall. The Mexican government was unhappy with foreign investors, and there were rumblings that the government was on the verge of confiscating the Cananea ranch. To protect stockholders' investments, Wiswall already had begun to expand the company's rangeland in the United States.

In November 1936, he called Sharp into his office. Wiswall had just acquired the sprawling Baca Float No. 5, and had learned that the 157,000-acre Mahon Ranch, adjoining the Baca Float's west boundary, was for sale. This ranch was "checkerboarded" between deeded and state-owned land. Wiswall knew that no one had ever successfully run the ranch; it was rough country and drought-prone, without well-developed stock waters. Nonetheless, he asked Sharp to travel to Arizona to study the feasibility of adding the Mahon Ranch to Baca Float No. 5.

Sharp returned with glowing reports of grass, browse and water on the ranch. Within the year, Wiswall had purchased the Mahon and sent Sharp back to Arizona to take over management of both ranches and operate them as the O RO Ranch.

Sharp eventually turned the two ranches into a well-watered and fenced cattle outfit with top-notch shipping pens and good housing for the crew. By 1939, the outfit reportedly ran 10,000 head of cattle, a formula that was bound to spell disaster on the unpredictable Arizona rangeland. Eventually droughts in the 1950s forced herd numbers to be cut to 5,500 head. Today, due to the continuing drought, cattle number less than half that amount.

Greene, the Son

Ranch management changed again in 1951 when Charles Greene, the colonel's son, replaced Sharp. Charles Greene and his stepfather, Charles Wiswall, had been running all the Arizona, California and Mexico Greene

Gathering horses is only a small part of Wes Foote's job description. He is cowboss on the ROs and wagon boss, as well.

Cisco Scott holds ends of two ropes as he and other cowboys circle the horses. He and his wife, Joni, have been at the ranch longer than any other employees.

ranches from the Greene Cattle Company office in Los Angeles, where the colonel had once lived part-time and had established his business office. When the ranching empire finally broke up in the 1950s, Charles Greene and his brother, Kirk, retained ownership of the O RO Ranch.

Mike McFarland, who went to work for the outfit as a teenager in the summer of 1965, remembered Charles and his wife, Sandy, as "wonderful" people. "Charlie was a really quiet man who was truly concerned about the men."

Some of the men Mike worked with in those days became Arizona legends. Such men as wagon boss Whistle Mills, Buck Smith, Ralph Chapman and Coley Lyons were Mike's mentors.

"It's a different age, alright," Mike explained. "Those guys were workhorses. They spent their whole lives living in tepees with the wagons, and they were tough. I don't care how bad the weather was, or how hot or how long the days. I was right out of high school, and they nearly killed me. I don't guess I ever worked with anybody who could gather the country any better than Whistle Mills. He knew how to work rough country

and trotty cattle, and he didn't leave any of his country unworked."

If anything conveys the work ethic and loyalty of these old-time cowboys, it's the story Mike told about Coley Lyons. Lyons had gone to work for the ROs before World War II, and was at the ranch until he died.

"I helped Coley move from the Triangle N Camp to headquarters when he decided he couldn't handle the work anymore," Mike recalled. "He told me a month before he gave it up, though, that he had one last thing he had to do, or he wouldn't feel like he had done his job. An old fence down in Cow Creek had been down before he went off to the war, and he had started rolling up this fence before he left. He never had gotten back down there to finish the job. But before he quit, he went back down there and rolled up that fence."

Dawn of a New Era

Today there's nothing left of the empire Colonel Greene built. In 1958, the Mexican government finally expropriated the Cananea Ranch. Charlie Wiswall died in 1952, and Mary in 1955. Charles Greene continued to manage the O RO Ranch until he became ill with terminal cancer. The ranch sold in 1973 to the JJJ Corporation, headed by John N. Irwin II and his family. This sale began a new era that continues today.

Born in 1913, Irwin had a distinguished political career, serving in the Defense Department under President Dwight D. Eisenhower, as a special ambassador to Panama and Peru under President Lyndon B. Johnson, as Deputy Secretary of State under President Richard M. Nixon and as ambassador to France from 1972 to 1973. Irwin's interest in owning an Arizona ranch was sparked by a summer spent working on a ranch as a boy, and by the fact that his grandfather was an early Arizona territorial governor.

Irwin died in 2000, but son John, daughter Jane Droppa and their families are carrying on the tradition. Droppa, who lives in Baltimore, Md., spends several months a year at the ranch with her husband, Larry, and their three children, Jack, Daniel and Katherine. As her father before her, Droppa loves being horseback and has a strong sense of responsibility for preserving the ranch's integrity.

Ranch Management

Operating a ranch the magnitude of the ROs is no easy undertaking. It requires a special person to juggle book work, range management, cattle operations and personnel.

Wayne Word, company president, has managed the ranch since 1993. He's a slim, wiry man with a boyish grin; only his silver-belly hat seems to set him apart from the rest of the cowboys. After graduating from Sul Ross State University at Alpine, Texas, Wayne, now 61, cowboyed and managed several smaller ranches and a feedlot before coming to the ROs. Admittedly he would rather be horseback than shuffling papers in his office, but he finds the opportunity to play both roles a real challenge.

"It's harder to keep your thumb on everything with a ranch this large, harder to find people who are capable of working in this kind of big country and a lot harder to manage as intensively as I was used to," he said. "Basically the O RO Ranch is run the same as it has been for the last 75 years, and probably what has enabled the ranch to survive is, for lack of a better word, economizing. The drought has been going on in Arizona for about 10 years, and it's been a challenge to try to survive with a lot fewer numbers. On the other hand, we'd rather struggle with that than hurt our range by overgrazing. In spite of the drought, I feel the range is in good condition now and will be able to recover quickly when we do get rain."

When Wayne came to the ranch, it was running 4,000 mother cows and 1,000 yearlings, too many, he thought, for the drought

Two cowhands contemplate the next move necessary to complete the day's work.

Water is
a most
precious
commodity
on the arid
Arizona
cattle ranch.

situation that had developed. His first management decision was to ship the steers and cut back the cow herd to 2,000 head. The cow herd at the time was mostly Beefmaster, which he believed were too large to be productive in this rough, rocky terrain, so he switched to Hereford and then Angus bulls. The ranch policy is to hold over weaned calves and sell them as yearlings.

With elevations varying from 4,000 to 6,000 feet, the ranch has a variety of feed and browse. Practically all the ranch water is supplied by dirt tanks. The original land grant is fenced into several large pastures, but the 157,000-acre west side, or Mahon, isn't cross-fenced. The lower country grows a lot of galletta grass and side-oats grama, while the upper country has more blue grama and a lot of browse, such as oak brush and mountain mahogany.

Camp Life at the ROs

Five camps are scattered around the ranch — Sandstone, Bear Creek, Francis Creek, Mahon and Triangle N. A cowboy lives at each of them year-round. His is strictly a riding job. He's responsible for his section of the country, which varies in size, depending on how rough the terrain is. A camp man keeps four horses and a couple of mules at his place for packing salt to places where he cannot go by truck.

"A good experienced camp man earns his money," Wayne said, "because he's constantly

Link Bundy, the Francis Creek camp man, brings a recalcitrant maverick to the pens.

A cowboy works through cattle penned at the headquarters on the Baca Float side of the ranch, one of only two places where cattle can be shipped.

moving cattle and checking the water and feed. He gets to know his country and the cattle located there. Part of his job is keeping his cattle gentle enough so we can gather them in the spring and fall."

Nowadays, compared to 20 years ago, the camps are fairly modern, with solar power and propane stoves and refrigerators, even televisions and cell phones. Camp accommodations vary from the cozy brick bungalow, nestled in a big grove of cottonwoods on pretty Francis Creek, to the yellowish-tan, wood-frame house, surrounded by juniper picket fences and corrals, in a malapai-strewn valley near Bear Creek. With most camps two hours or more from town, camp life is not easy on married men with families. Children generally must be home-schooled, and wives must find ways to entertain themselves in very isolated situations.

When she married Cisco Scott and moved to the Mahon Camp 20 years ago, Joni, his wife, the daughter of an Elko, Nev., cattle trader, was no stranger to living in the country. This couple has been at the ranch longer than any other employees, unlike many camp people who tend to move from job to job. At 48, Joni admits that not having children has made their lifestyle easier, but sees no hardship in her chosen life. The Scotts lived at Mahon, the most remote camp on the ranch, for seven years before moving to Bear Creek. Though only 30 miles from headquarters, the road to Mahon is so rough and rocky, and often washed out, that it takes more than two hours to make the drive, plus another hour after that to get to town. Needless to say, the Scotts made the trip only about twice a month.

"You just couldn't afford to drive your vehicle in there," Joni said, speaking in a tiny voice, her long black hair gathered in a braid. "In the winter we'd leave our truck at headquarters and pack everything in on mules."

Even at Bear Creek Camp, only an hour from headquarters, people have been snowed in for more than a month, and more than once. Several years ago, when it snowed more than two feet, the Scotts scraped by on groceries, but Cisco had to ride out with the pack mules to get oats for the horses.

Cattle work in the ROs pens can be dry, dusty and dirty, yet satisfying to those with an affinity for horses and cattle.

Joni doesn't profess to be a cowgirl, but rides with Cisco on occasion "just for fun." She stays busy sewing, reading, gardening and walking with their Border Collie, Stonewall—dogs are not allowed at the wagon. On occasion, when the wagon has been without a cook, Joni has filled in, carrying food to where the wagon was camped. At Mahon, she had only an antique, wood-burning stove, but at Bear Creek, there is a wood stove and the luxury of a gas stove, as well. In winter she prefers the wood stove for the extra warmth it provides.

Despite the occasional hardships, Joni would not trade any of her life for town. "It's an incredible luxury to live on a ranch that's mostly private land," she said. "The things you see — bobcats, eagles, coyotes. You can't see those things in town. I guess if you like to be outside and you like animals, then you're endlessly entertained here."

Life on the Wagon

The main thing that sets the O RO Ranch apart from other big Arizona outfits is that the ROs runs a roundup wagon for both the spring and fall works. The old mule-drawn wagon from earlier days still rests under a cluster of oak trees at headquarters, but today's "modern" wagon is actually an old World War II, six-by-six army truck that easily gets across the rough country as the crew moves from one area of the ranch to another.

Usually about 10 cowboys ride with the wagon, including the regular camp men and the cowboss, Wes Foote, who lives at headquarters. Foote, tall and lean as a hound, often wears a black hat, the hallmark of the Arizona cowboy. At 28, he's young for his position, but he's also the wagon boss. His brother, Toby, who lives at Sandstone, is the jigger boss, or second-in-command, when the wagon is out. Finding help for the wagon is not always easy, said Wes, who must put together a crew and get the cattle worked. He also oversees the remuda and makes sure all the camp men have what they need when the wagon is not out.

"It's tough to find sure-enough, really good cowboys," he said. "Not that there aren't a lot of good hands out there, but it's changed so much. A lot of young guys know they can make a better living somewhere else. It's difficult to find anybody who wants to go on the wagon like this and who's still enough of a hand to be of some help to you. I'm not

Cowboss Wes Foote drags a calf to be worked at the Burro Mesa Tank.

saying I don't want to help somebody learn if they really want to, but it's sure not a babysitting kind of outfit."

Cowboys must supply their own shoeing tools, tack, bedrolls and tepees. Each man is assigned eight horses from the 100-head remuda. He generally rides two horses a day, changing at midday when they "noon out" for lunch.

The spring wagon is out from approximately May 1 to the end of June, when the cowboys brand calves and wean the late calves that had been turned out for the winter. Then, from September 1 to late November, the crew weans calves, picks up bulls, culls cows and ships yearlings, getting ready for winter.

Cattle can be shipped from only two areas on the ROs— Francis Creek Camp on the far western border of the Mahon and at the headquarters on the Baca Float side of the ranch. Everything shipped must be brought to one of those two places, and the crew might have to drive the cattle 15 to 20 miles. This could take three to four days so, during a drive, the crew drops the cattle into overnight traps scattered around the ranch, then picks them up and moves on the next morning.

Young men, often from other parts of the country, typically seek work to hone their skills at long-established outfits such as the ROs.

Branding on the ROs can be a two-fisted proposition.

There is ample seating for the lunch crowd working cattle at Antelope Tank.

The Wagon Cook

Next to the cowboys, the cook is the wagon's most indispensable man during the spring and fall works. Cooks willing to live in a tepee and cook outside in any kind of weather are becoming about as rare as gold coins. Wayne Word guesses the ranch has been through some 14 cooks in the 14 years he has been there. Cooks have ranged from a cowboy talked into cooking for better pay to a guy hiding out from a driving-under-the-influence charge, to another who rode in on a bicycle from the Louisiana oilfields. Some lasted only a couple of days.

When Leonard McNab showed up two wagons ago, he was a godsend. Lenny, as the cowboys call him, was headed from his native New Hampshire to the bright lights of Las Vegas when his dilapidated truck broke down in Winslow. Somehow he wound up packing mules at the Grand Canyon and met a young cowboy who was headed for the ROs wagon. Lenny tagged along in search of a new adventure.

Lenny's eyes sparkle behind horn-rimmed glasses on his round face, a black derby hat perched jauntily on his head. A robust figure in his denim overalls and "old-time cookie" shirt, as he calls it, he's quick with a smile or

An Arizona cowhand takes a break at West Split.

a laugh, and has fit in easily with the wagon. As is the coyote in Ian Tyson's song, "The Coyote and the Cowboy," Lenny is a conundrum; he has studied French cooking in Germany, reads Kurt Vonnegut, plays a mean Johnny Cash on the guitar and can quote from Homer's *Odyssey*.

He chuckles when he recalls his job interview. "So Wes says to me, 'Leonard, what are you going to bring to the table here?'"

"And I said, 'Well, I'll bring food to the table. I don't have a punchy bone in my body, so that's about all I can do.' Then I said, 'You know, you can't trust a skinny cook.'"

Lenny got the job. He did not know a thing about cooking with Dutch ovens, but he learned fast. The ROs is one of the last of the "pot-rack" outfits in existence. During good weather everything is cooked outside in Dutch ovens over coals, an art that is all but lost today. In bad weather the cook attaches a tent onto the back of the wagon and cooks on a wood-burning, portable stove.

The cowboys butcher a beef once every two weeks or so, if the weather isn't too hot, and leave it hanging in a juniper tree with a tarp cover. Meals traditionally consist of fried steak (while the steaks last), goulash, barbecued beef, tamale pie, beans, fried potatoes, biscuits and cobbler. Lenny has taken the repertoire a notch higher, offering such gourmet delicacies as sauerbraten, prime rib with sweet onion and shitake mushroom sauce, and even quiche.

"I tell them it's egg pie," he said with a smile.

Two other positions on the wagon, the horse wrangler and the "hood," are becoming virtually extinct; few youngsters are willing to take on these tasks. The hood is a cook's helper, who generally cuts wood, washes dishes and does whatever other menial tasks the cook needs to have done. Years ago, a kid who wanted to be a cowboy worked his way up, from the hood job to working around the branding pen, flanking calves and, eventually, doing more and more until he became an accomplished hand. Such boys were called "hoodlums" because they were usually homeless, knock-about kids with nowhere to go.

The RO Horses

In early November, the wagon camps at Francis Creek, its last leg before the fall works end. Francis Creek is one of the few wagon camps set next to a camp house. At this high-desert elevation, deep in the canyon, the fall air is warm and the cottonwood leaves

The "jig line," as it is called, heads back to camp when the work is complete.

Cactus and roacks are constant companions on the remote Arizona ranch.

still cling to the trees in a last burst of gold and yellow. Most of the crew rest in their tepees after a long day's work. Tired saddle horses rest, too, in the creek bottom after a day of "rock-pounding." Many of the horses wear pieces of old jeans tied around their pasterns as makeshift bell boots for protection from the rocky terrain.

A couple of cowboys wrangle the next day's horses out of the adjacent pasture. Out of habit, the horses know to drift down the trail to water. The "honest" ones head down the hill, even from the back corner of the pasture, at the mere sight of wranglers; these horses know the routine. Only a few renegades try to hang back until forced to come.

Once all 100 or so horses are trapped in the big corral below the camp house, the cowboys silently circle them in the center of the pen. Each man tosses the end of his rope to the man to his right until they have formed a rope circle around the herd. This ritual is repeated morning, noon and night. The horses have learned to bunch together and not try to escape as the wagon boss and jigger boss throw houlihan loops over horses' heads. Each man calls out the name of the

two horses he will use the following day—"Redbird," "Lonesome," "Creature," "Circus" and so on until all are caught and led to a holding corral.

The 20 or so horses to be used the next day are then turned into a smaller pasture to be wrangled the next morning when the "drive" horses are caught. One man then stays behind to drive the "afternoon" horses out to wherever the crew is nooned-out for lunch. After the crew catches their fresh horses, he drives the morning horses back to camp.

The RO horses have been renowned from the very beginning of the ranch's history. Some of the Cananea horses naturally came north to form the remuda and broodmare herd at the Arizona ranch. Old-timers still remember them as some of the best ranch horses they ever rode.

That tradition continues today. Keeping enough horses for the remuda is a big job, so the ranch runs about 30 broodmares and three stallions. The remuda consists of 100 to 110 geldings, and everything is still branded with an RO.

"Because our country is so rough and rocky, we have to raise our own horses,"

Wayne explained. "You can't go out and buy horses because they just get crippled and don't hold up. We demand a lot of our horses, so we're very particular about correctness, soundness and good feet and withers. The horses also have to be a decent size to handle roping 1,000-pound cattle at times. There's an advantage to raising these horses outside in this big country — they just develop better."

In the past, colts were quickly halter-broken as weanlings, then turned out and never touched again until they were started as 3-year-olds. Today the halter-breaking and handling process is more intense, with several reminder sessions between weaning and age 3. Those sessions make training the colts much easier later.

In recent years, Wayne has begun infusing modern bloodlines into the old foundation mares forming the broodmare band nucleus. Current stallions include Dual Winner, by Dual Peppy; TRR Janies Playgun, by Playgun; and Peppy Smooth Scoot, a grandson of Mr San Peppy. The ranch usually keeps all the geldings it raises, but sells any fillies that are not kept as broodmare replacements.

Looking to the Future

When Bob Sharp took over management of the O RO Ranch in 1937, he rode to the top of Mount Hope to better grasp the rangeland's magnitude. He "sat motionless in wonder. There spread out before me, under a cloudless sea-blue sky, was a tremendous span of bright, clear, serene rangeland—one that was still pure," he wrote.

Cowboss Wes Foote has been there, too. He spoke quietly, struggling to express his feelings. "There's a lot of country, pretty rough old country...it's just that kind of ranch. But that's one of the reasons I like it. It wouldn't be the same if it was easy, I guess. It's a cowboy deal and a horseback deal, and

O RO Ranch Timeline

1821: The Spanish crown granted Don Luis Maria Baca 500,000 acres near Los Alamos, N.M.

1856: Following the Gadsden Purchase, the U.S. government agreed to "float" the land-grant rights of Don Luis' heirs to five 100,000-acre tracts, one north of Prescott, Ariz.

1880: San Francisco land speculator Dr. Edward B. Perrin purchased the Baca Float No. 5, and his son, Lilo Perrin, managed the land until 1936.

1901: Colonel William Cornell Greene formed the Greene Cattle Company north of the U.S.-Mexican border and the Cananea Cattle Company in Mexico. Greene registered the "OR" brand in the United States and the "RO" brand in Mexico.

1911: Before Greene died as a result of a buggy accident, he entrusted his family and his ranch holdings to Charles Wiswall, who later married Greene's widow.

1936: Greene Cattle Company purchased Baca Float No. 5, and Wiswall asked Greene's son-in-law, Robert L. Sharp, to check out the adjoining 157,000-acre Mahon Ranch, which was purchased, as well. Sharp then managed the combined outfits as the O RO Ranch.

1940: J. Ernest Browning inspected more than 900 head of Greene Cattle Company horses and selected 250 prime mares and stallions to register with the fledgling American Quarter Horse Association.

1951: Colonel Greene's son, Charles Green, began managing the "ROs," as the ranch became known, and he and his brother retained ranch ownership when the cattle company empire broke up later that decade.

1973: The O RO Ranch sold to the JJJ Corporation, headed by John N. Irwin II and his family.

1993: Wayne Word, now president of the ranching company, hired on to manage the ROs.

2000: John N. Irwin II passed away, but his son, John, and daughter, Jane Droppa, continue to operate the ranch.

there will always be something that needs doing with a cow. The key is having owners who appreciate what they have."

Fortunately for Foote and his kind, the Droppa and Irwin families have no intention of changing anything. Hopefully, the ROs always will be home for men who still know the ways of a cow and a horse, and don't mind putting in a hard day's work close to land that is pure and unaltered by civilization.

"Ol' Bud is just like
John Wayne to us ...
there ain't anybody better."
Buddy Adams

3

ADAMS
RANCH

By Tim O'Byrne

A steady stream of traffic whistles past the Adams Ranch sign on Highway 68 west of Fort Pierce, Fla. The dangerously narrow blacktop requires a driver's full attention, leaving him little time to admire small groups of red cattle contentedly grazing in well-fenced, roadside pastures.

The scene deserves more than a passing glance from the window of a moving pickup. Aside from its pastoral beauty, south-central Florida holds a special place in American ranching's long, colorful history.

Here, on the native-inhabited peninsula's western coast in 1521, Spanish explorer Juan Ponce de Leon offloaded some of the first cattle onto what would someday become the United

Ranching in Florida might seem a paradise to some until they encounter the fog, heat and humidity.

Riding in the rain is part of a Florida cowboy's life, and a slicker often is necessary attire.

States of America. In essence, the motley herd of compact, distinctly marked, Andalusian-bred cows comprised the seed stock that one day would mature into a multibillion-dollar industry encompassing all 50 states and boasting 100 million head of cattle. Today, almost 500 years later, the American rancher produces 25 billion pounds of beef annually and exports it to every continent on earth.

Adams family members have come to be recognized as exemplary cattlemen, as well as environmental leaders. Their story could easily be a great American testimonial to hard work, perseverance and an unselfish dedication to Mother Earth that burns strongly in any true naturalist's heart.

The Land Nobody Wanted

Bud Adams knows every inch of his family's 65,000-acre Florida cattle ranch scattered across three divisions in St. Lucie, Okeechobee and Osceola Counties. In addition to the ranch cattle operation, diversification efforts have resulted in a citrus division that grows both oranges and grapefruit.

Few Florida cowboys ride out to work cattle without a slicker tied on the saddle.

Adams Ranch cowboys ride sorrels from the outfit's evenly matched remuda.

Articulate and witty, Bud, a Southern gentleman, exudes great wisdom gleaned from decades of thoughtful observation, and those around him soon come to appreciate his passion for life.

An old black-and-white photograph of Bud, born Alto Adams Jr., was taken sometime during the Great Depression. The photo is among a multitude of framed images displayed in the spacious ranch office's second story.

The then-young lad of 12, dressed and ready to put in a day's work with the cracker cowboys, sits on the cattle pen's top rail. The pen holds 600-pound, authentic Florida Cracker cattle, remnants of a breed descended from the original Spanish cattle, which stubbornly had dominated the state's piney woods and flat prairies for more than four centuries. The image is powerful because, at the time, the cattle captured behind the glass plate almost had been bred out of existence, although the historic strain has since experienced resurgence in popularity. The boy watching cattle in the photograph has since grown into a respected keeper of the past and purveyor of the future.

Today, Bud prowls the ranch in a sport utility vehicle's relative comfort, his professional-quality digital camera at the ready in the center console. Nothing escapes his keen eye.

"My father got the chance to buy this land from a speculator in Iowa," Bud explained. "It was the end of the Depression, and that speculator wanted out pretty badly, because nobody wanted to buy it. The land was deemed worthless."

Bud's father, Alto Adams Sr., had a different vision. Alto, the son of a Civil War orphan, and his family were no strangers to hard times on the farm. When Alto came of age, his father offered him 40 acres and a mule to make a start in life. But the enterprising young man had his own ideas and asked instead to trade the mule and land for tuition to the University of Florida.

His wish was granted, and several years later Alto became a hard-working lawyer in Fort Pierce, just 12 miles east of the present-day ranch site. Alto's practice flourished, and his business ventures matured, one of them the ranch property he had acquired for $1.25 an acre from the desperate speculator. A measure of pity goes to the speculator's heirs—surrounding real estate today can easily fetch $25,000 per acre for "the land nobody wanted."

Florida Crackers

"We're called Florida crack-uhs down here," explains an Adams Ranch veteran in a deep Southern drawl.

Just as the Southwest hands refer to themselves as "cowpunchers" and the Great Basin guys call themselves "buckaroos," the term "cracker" was adopted by the southern horse-back cattle-handlers, descendents of predominately English settlers who moved into Florida during the 19th century. The name's origin is based on their unique style of gathering and working free-roaming cattle—using the crack of a 12-foot whip to move the herds.

A Florida cracker cowboy makes cracking the whip look easy, but to do it right takes a

Alligators are an ever-present consideration on the Florida cattle ranch.

Jenna Adams, Billy's daughter and an accomplished horsewoman, first began working with the ranch crew at age 7 or so.

really good whip, a lot of practice, and a great deal of finesse. *How* to crack it, especially when sitting on a nice, forgiving ranch horse that trusts the rider aboard to take care of him, is one thing. *When* to crack it is yet another. The best crackers understand that constantly using the whip's amazing sound eventually desensitizes cattle, annoys horses and does little to ease the stress of daily cow work.

Cowboy crews working big, rough country constantly need to stay in sync with one another for a successful gather. High-desert buckaroo crews, spread across several miles of open sagebrush country, wear bright red or white shirts to make it easier for riders in adjacent circles to see them at great distances. Each mountain cowboy working the high country has a signature yell he uses to let other crewmembers know where he is when they are separated by thick timber or deep draws. When a cowboy unleashes his particular yell at the top of his lungs, he means to let the others know his position, and, in turn, expects to be answered so he can pinpoint where the others are.

Likewise, the versatile cracker whip performs a similar and valuable function. Florida crackers spend their days working in thick vegetation or heavy rainfall, which limits vision and cannot easily be penetrated by anyone's signature yell. So, instead, the southern cowboys rely on the rifle-like whip cracks to let their approximate whereabouts be known during a cattle gather.

Cattle Paradise

At one time Cracker cattle were the bovines best-suited to survive the deceptive south-central Florida environment. Warm ocean breezes, sunny days with high clouds and seemingly lush vegetation year-round often lull the newcomer into believing that cow paradise exists between the Sunshine State's idyllic shores.

It does, but not without a price. Northern cattlemen routinely face bitter winters, frozen water tanks, late spring grass, drought, grasshoppers and enormous hay costs. These ranchers might cast envious eyes toward their Floridian counterparts, unaware of the challenges their Southern neighbors battle any given year.

Florida seems to take almost as much as it gives. Wildly unpredictable weather can dish out hurricane devastation in the summer, a grass-killing frost in winter, severe flooding or, unbelievably to most not acquainted with the state, lengthy periods of drought that deplete surface water and Florida's shallow underground aquifer.

Zachary Adams, Mike's son, graduated from the University of Florida with an agricultural degree and works full-time on the ranch.

Alligators, whose populations have increased dramatically since the 1930s, infest inland waterways. Rarely do they take a calf, but, in addition to birds and small mammals, the insatiable monsters, given the opportunity, dine on humans, as well. Poisonous snakes, such as the water moccasin, swim the dark water without fear, and one of the largest rattlesnake species in North America slithers and hides among the dense foliage.

Bloodthirsty mosquitoes create a living nightmare for cattle and horses, and mosquito-borne malaria in humans has been confirmed as recently as 2003 in nearby Okeechobee County. Bud Adams actually contracted the potentially fatal disease in the 1950s but, with the help of modern medicine, recovered. Such parasites as ticks, lice and worms abound, and internally damaging liver flukes infect the pasture vegetation that cattle readily consume.

Then there is the summer heat coupled with an almost suffocating relative humidity. Tallying the negative aspects of Florida cattle ranching brings things into perspective, dashing all thoughts of a cow paradise in the minds of any visiting cattlemen.

Venerable Cracker Cattle

The original Florida Cracker cattle survived in such circumstances for more than four centuries, primarily because of their sinewy adaptability, but the breed could not compete with bovine genetic advances occurring in other parts of the country. Things were headed for a major change.

In 1944, Bud Adams joined the U.S. Navy and sailed away during the final days of World War II. After his service discharge, Bud attended the University of Florida, graduating with degrees in commerce and business administration. In 1948, when he returned to manage the ranch, he clearly had his hands full.

The mass war exodus of working-age men had created a headache for ranchers nationwide, especially in south-central Florida, where hardy, small-framed Cracker cattle were really only one lightning storm away from reverting to their feral natures. With few men to tend them during that time, Adams Ranch cattle had become noticeably wilder and far less reliant on human intervention.

"We roped and tied many a slick 3-year-old bull in those days after the war," Bud recalled of the post-war, mop-up exercise.

With a nation demanding top-quality beef for the dinner table, and a ranch just rolling in green grass, Bud knew he must make significant genetic modifications to the Adams herd to give consumers what they wanted. Cracker cattle simply did not meet the standard when it came to carcass grading, and earlier attempts to introduce Brahman strains proved successful to a point, but the plan seemed to just miss the mark.

A Long, Genetic Trail

Bud's deep interest in cattle genetics and vegetative improvement began to blossom at this critical point. His father, appointed Chief Justice of the Florida Supreme Court in 1949, had relocated to Tallahassee, leaving Bud in charge of the Fort Pierce outfit. Bud's strategy was to bring in new blood and develop a cow that could meet marketplace demands.

With his father sitting on the bench in Tallahassee, Bud's new responsibility was to make the ranch enterprise viable, but it takes a great deal of time and effort to build a cow herd from scratch. However, the Adams Ranch went much farther down the trail than most, meticulously developing an entirely

Adam Smith and his ranch horse offered a young calf a lift back to the pens.

The cattle are fresh and frisky despite shirtsleeve temperatures and obvious high humidity.

Billy Adams, cowboss on the St. Lucie division of the ranch, demonstrated how the "cracker" cowboy came by his name.

new breed of cattle to fit the unique Florida environment.

"We brought some purebred Hereford bulls to use on our Brahman cow herd," Bud explained. "But the Hereford sires by themselves passed on to the calves certain physical characteristics that were not desirable for our conditions."

One of those traits is white-eye pigment. In nature's complex choreography, dark pigment around the cattle's eyes results in fewer eye-related illnesses or afflictions, such as ocular cancer and pinkeye. To circumvent this minor obstacle, Bud continued with the Hereford influence, but primarily on the paternal side, creating a sleek, crossbred bull with the best of both Brahman and Hereford characteristics.

After two long decades of calculated breeding in the Adams Ranch's closed environs, the Braford cattle breed was officially chartered in 1969. Creating a chartered breed of registered cattle, one that has grown steadily in popularity to this day, is no insignificant feat, but Bud is quick to brush off much of the credit for his visionary work.

"I'd like to say it was my idea all along," he confessed, "but the whole thing was really born of necessity."

The goals were to create a cow herd that not only would be easy to handle, breed, calve out and tend, but also one that would deliver better quality meat to the consumer. One look at the present-day Adams Ranch herds raising their calves on nearby pastureland is proof enough that 60 years of careful selection and meticulous attention to detail most certainly have paid dividends.

Ranch visitors, who appreciate what it takes to visualize a new cattle breed and commit to developing a seed herd, take their time when looking through the Adams' Brafords. The mother-cow herd produces 7,000 calves annually. Through careful selection, not always guided by the hand of man, each and every animal in today's herd has earned the right to fan out contentedly across the flat grassland or shade up in a hammock, or treed knoll, nearby.

Since 1969, Adams Ranch Brafords have served as the foundation herd for this hardy breed that enjoys worldwide popularity. Although Bud does not dismiss his early successes, and always will remain loyal to Brafords, his genetic vision has since taken a new direction.

ABEEF is a composite cross of heat-tolerant cattle that Bud and his crew have been developing since 1990. Their work is based on a scientifically supported breeding program and draws on studies conducted at the Meat Animals Research Center in Clay Center, Neb. The predominately red cattle are a composite of Red Angus, Gelbvieh, Hereford and Brahman lineage.

Vegetative Changes

Master cattlemen and range graziers are patient, observant individuals. Back when the intricacies of the environmental rangeland puzzle were first being unraveled, old-school range reports did not incorporate computer-generated models and infrared photography. Instead, data gathering relied on a pair of eagle eyes, the willingness to stay in one spot indefinitely while in the field and watch closely, and an open mind, one that has spent far more time pondering possibilities than rejecting assumptions.

Developing a new cattle breed to replace the hardy Cracker cattle, which had flourished on the peninsula for centuries, was difficult. This new breed needed to eat to gain weight and produce meat, but the native range grasses that sustained the Cracker cattle weren't enough to satiate Braford appetites. The grasses were too high in water content and too low in nutritional value. This time, the environment had to change to support the cattle, and at this crossroads, the Adams Ranch reset the ecosystem bar.

"We did a lot of homework and collaborated with the University of Florida to introduce a better selection of nutritious plants," Bud explained.

Legumes and clovers were popular choices, and a variety of hemarthria grass called floralta, imported in the 1980s from South Africa, impressed Bud and his colleagues immensely. But how can any rancher with a limited budget and a tight work schedule maintain a fiscal conscience when the margins between survival and sell-off are slim? Here is where the road less traveled became

The Adams Ranch is known for creating the Braford breed, as well as for being an outstanding steward of natural resources in a somewhat fragile environment.

Most ranch-raised fillies are halter-broken and sold during the ranch's annual cattle-production sale.

the most attractive route for the enterprising Adams family.

Mother Nature's Stewards

When a mid-1960s national obsession with chemical applications and aggressive environment intervention became the norm in this ever-changing industry, the Adams Ranch refrained from using pesticides to kill insect outbreaks. Instead, the Adamses encouraged Mother Nature, in her own subtle but powerful way, to exercise both her might and light touch, balancing and correcting that which required those things.

Irrigation ditches, useful 20th-century tools installed on the ranch at great capital expense to alleviate drought cycles, are alive with minnows that feed on mosquito larvae. Large fish feed on the minnows, and birds of prey, such as eagles and osprey, feed on the fish.

Land that has been drained and reclaimed by the irrigation ditches grows both range grass and brush. In the past, fire had been put to work to keep brush in check, as well, but deer by the hundreds now do so, browsing alongside graz-ing cattle in the evening and early morning hours in a truly symbiotic relationship.

In south-central Florida, a hammock is a relatively small, thick stand of diverse trees and vegetation situated on ground that is slightly, sometimes only inches, higher than the surrounding grasslands or wetlands. The origin of the term, generally believed to mean "a place of shade," likely came from the Taino people native to the Dominican Republic when the Spanish arrived. Now wild Florida hammocks are becoming rare as development continues to claim the native lands.

The Adams Ranch is among a select group of conservation-minded entities recognized for saving the Florida hammock from obliteration. Controlled cattle grazing actually contributes to hammock proliferation, as the cows shade up under the hammock's canopy. Cattle droppings supply nutrients to the surrounding soil, which, in turn, feeds the vegetation supported by the hammock.

It seems as if everything—hammocks, deer, cattle and fish—is supposed to be here on the ranch, together at this one time. The Adamses, caretakers of the land, understand that concept, and aim to keep things this way.

Something special happened many decades ago on this ranch, at a time when the term "stewards of the land" had never been part of ranching's vocabulary. For visionaries such as Bud, environmental protection on the family ranch became more than a buzzword; the Adamses literally must live with any mistakes they might make.

In recognition of the Adams Ranch philosophy and its dedication to environmentalism in the true sense of the word, the National Cattlemen's Association awarded Bud its first Environmental Award for the outfit's stewardship of the fragile south-central Florida ecosystem. The 1991 recognition was two-fold; the Florida Cattlemen's Association awarded its own Environmental Award to the Adams Ranch, as well, thereby sealing the deal with state and national applause. America's cattle industry leaders watched it all happen, took notes, and then returned to their respective outfits, resolved to make equally significant environmental changes of their own.

A Hard-to-Leave Outfit

When asked if he has trouble finding and retaining help, a common problem endemic these days in large-scale commercial agriculture, ranch owner Bud responded with a wide grin, "Trouble finding any help? Heck, I can't get 'em to leave!"

A good example of an Adams Ranch "lifer," or long-term employee, is Buddy Adams, manager of the St. Lucie Ranch and an accomplished performance horseman, as well as a knowledgeable cowman. Buddy is no relation to Bud and, in fact, had never heard of him until hauling a friend's horse to the outfit more than 40 years ago.

"I took one look at the outfit and said, 'Man, I'd like to spend some of my time out here,'" Buddy recalled with a smile. "I've raised my kids here, and now we have some grandkids coming up, too, who want to stick around."

Buddy's son, Billy, is cow boss of the St. Lucie division, and together with a great crew of long-term crackers loyal to the Adams brand, they make sure everything rolls along smoothly.

All Adams Ranch divisions use horses to gather and pen cattle. During branding, however, they do not drag calves to the fire. They must be separated from the cows anyway, as they are run through the chutes and dewormed, a common practice on many American ranches.

The cracker cowboy crew might trailer or trot their horses to cattle, depending on the task. The crew makes a lot of miles horseback, given the ranch's size, and it takes time, working among the hammocks and canals, to select routes and navigate water-crossings. A typical summer day starts early with a 3 a.m. breakfast, simply because cattle do not work well in the humid heat encountered around 10 a.m. and beyond. Nonetheless, the cracker cowboys work effectively as they ride for the brand of their choice.

Buddy best summed up why hands seldom leave the Adams outfit: "Old' Bud is just like John Wayne to us … there ain't anybody better."

From Crackers to Quarters

Every contemporary photograph of Adams Ranch cracker cowboys seems to have one thing in common—they all ride sorrel horses. Horses raised in the area seem to better tolerate the mosquitoes and bugs than do horses brought in from other regions. Muck itch, also

Just as the Great Basin has its buckaroos, Florida ranching country has its crackers.

On occasion, Adam Smith must tie his horse and climb atop the chute to work cattle.

The Adams Ranch remuda now boasts an evenly matched collection of sorrel geldings from a dynamic set of American Quarter Horse Association Appendix-registered mares. The mares resulted from breeding ranch Quarter Horses to a ranch-owned Thoroughbred stallion. The ranch-raised mares were then bred to the ranch stallion, Mr Dry Eyes, a son of Peppy San Badger, purchased as a 2-year-old in 2003.

"We visited the King Ranch," Buddy Adams recalled, "and we liked the horses they raised—good ranch using horses with great feet. We decided to buy one of their young studs, and he's worked out just fine for us."

The Adams outfit liked the resulting horses' size, withers and the sturdy legs and feet that allow ranch mounts to make long circles. In 2006, for example, the ranch weaned 21 foals, and most fillies are halter-broken and sold during the ranch's annual cattle-production sale. But selling horses is not necessarily the priority. The outfit consistently raises the best horses possible to do the necessary ranch work and often keeps both young and mature horses in the remuda.

"We start colts when they're 2," Buddy explained, "and we like to [ground] drive 'em at first. Then we get on and get 'em riding, maybe make a few short circles taking cattle back to pasture."

Ranch cowboys don't push colts much as 2-year-olds, but ride them progressively more as they mature into 4-year-olds. By that point, the sorrel geldings are pretty much ready to join the ranch work force.

"To us," Buddy added, "the horse is a tool we use to pen cattle. Everyone likes to use a sharp tool, so we breed and train to make them the best we can."

The Family Tradition

No doubt, the Florida cattle ranch will remain firmly in the Adams family's control. More than 30 family members from three generations have an interest in the ranch, now a family-owned corporation

Bud and his wife, Dot, have three sons, and each has taken a role in the business. Mike is the company president, Lee (Alto III) is vice president of cattle operations, and Robert is in charge of the citrus division. The three sons reside on the ranch, as does Bud's sister, Elaine Harrison, whose

known as sweet itch, is a common Florida equine skin ailment, which often must be tolerated alongside the insects.

Through the years the ranch has drifted away from using the traditional cracker horse, but ranch manager Buddy Adams can recall throwing a leg over the real deal not that long ago. A cracker horse, typically solid-colored, ranges 13.5 to 15 hands in height and weighs between 700 and 1,000 pounds. Some cracker horses also had a gait called the "coon rack," somewhat akin to a fast walk. According to Buddy, who rode such horses as a young man, a cracker horse could not outrun a cow, but could outlast her—a testament to the horse's endurance.

As Cracker cattle were replaced with larger breeds, the cracker ponies could no longer hold the heavier cattle that required roping and doctoring. Bigger cows called for bigger horses, so change began in the 1940s, and the ranch began using primarily Quarter Horses and Quarter-crosses.

As is the case with such legendary outfits, the Adams brand has been in use for many years.

Adams Ranch Timeline

1899: Alto L. Adams was born in the Florida Panhandle. He and his wife, Carra Williams, married in 1925 and had two children, Alto Jr. (Bud) and Elaine.

1937: Alto Sr. paid $1.25 an acre for a huge tract of open range-land west of Fort Pierce, Fla., which become the 65,000-acre Adams Ranch, with holdings in three counties.

1948: After serving in the U.S. Navy and graduating from the University of Florida, Bud Adams became a partner in Alto Adams and Son, moved to the ranch and managed the operation while his father served on the Florida State Supreme Court.

1948 – 1963: The father-and-son team of Alto Sr. and Bud expanded ranch holdings, working diligently to develop the cow herd and grazing land, yet remaining committed to sustaining south-central Florida's fragile, yet complex ecosystem.

1959: Bud was elected Florida Cattlemen's Association president.

1963: The Adams Ranch was incorporated with owners listed as Alto (Bud) Adams Jr. and Elaine Adams Harrison, and their respective children.

1969: The Adams family was instrumental in founding the International Braford Association, now known as United Braford Breeders, and Adams Ranch registered Braford cattle are recognized as the breed's foundation herd.

1970 – 1978: Bud and Dot's three sons, Michael, Alto III (Lee) and Robert joined their father to run their respective portions of the ranching enterprise.

1989: Alto Adams Sr. passed away.

1991: The ranch received the National Cattlemen's Beef Association Stewardship Award and the Environmental Award from the Florida Cattlemen's Association.

1999: NCBA recognized the Adams Ranch as Ranch of the Century.

son, Peter, works on the ranch as an acting vice president. Long-term employee Dianne Haenning makes sure the office is running efficiently each day.

The youngest members of this fourth-generation ranching family are just now looking beyond formal educations toward life lessons that can be learned by working alongside their elders. If ever a rancher were to be blessed, it would be by living long enough to see the outfit glide effortlessly into the hands of deserving children and grandchildren.

"It's important for us to create and maintain the kind of environment that the next generation will want to be a part of," Bud explained, while casting a glance toward the not-too-distant future. With so many willing grandchildren nearby, it appears as though Bud and his sister, Elaine, are among those fortunately blessed.

The Adams Ranch's amazing story is not only about developing cattle breeds, winning environmental awards or even surviving in an economically challenging industry, where profit margins can evaporate like Florida's morning mist. It also is about how one family has stuck together through the decades to make their little corner of the world something worthy of protecting and inspiring to others.

The visionary family's astute choices have helped stimulate the collective conscience of today's American ranchers. The Adamses have set the bar for the manner in which cattle, horses, humans and the most fragile of ecosystems can co-exist and thrive. The Adams Ranch belongs here, and if luck remains on Florida's side, it will still be here a hundred years from now.

> *"Riding a good horse surrounded by beautiful scenery doesn't feel like work to me. And I get to do it all over again the next day."*
> **Roger Peters**

4

DRAGGING Y CATTLE CO.

By Guy de Galard

Roger Peters loves what he does for a living.
"I never worked a day in my life," he declared, joking. "Riding a good horse surrounded by beautiful scenery doesn't feel like work to me. And I get to do it all over again the next day."

However, his hard work, perseverance and wise decisions have made the Dragging Y one of the most successful outfits in his region of Montana.

In 1973, Roger and his wife, Carrie, moved from Colorado to help his father run a ranch he had acquired in southwestern Montana, near Whitehall. After purchasing a Montana brand from an old cowboy, a "Y" with a short tail, Roger has managed

During the fall drive, the 1,850-head cattle herd stretches more than 3 miles.

61

to combine several desirable ranches into the Dragging Y and now owns what he considers some of the best grassland in Beaverhead County. This land of spacious valleys, wide vistas and lush mountain meadows surrounded by majestic mountain ranges is considered the last bastion of Montana's historic and large working cattle ranches.

A Regional Overview

Montana's commercial cattle business began here in the state's southwestern corner, where high meadows meet the Continental Divide at the outermost reaches of the Missouri River's watershed. This is prime cattle country, thanks to an abundance of snow-fed mountain streams. This also was a region of gold mining camps, prime markets for beef. Texas Longhorns were trailed north in the late 1860s, and more than 130 years later Beaverhead County leads the state in total cattle numbers.

The country around the Dragging Y is open, with magnificent views of the Pioneer and Black Tail ranges. Just over one of the ridges surrounding the ranch is Bannack, an 1860s ghost town that has retained the atmosphere of its dark days when crooked sheriff Henry Plummer and his gang of road agents terrorized the nearby gold camps. By some accounts, there never was a mining town of

the same size that contained more desperadoes and highwaymen than did Bannack during the winter of 1862 through '63.

More to the Southwest, the snowcapped peaks of the Bitterroot and Beaverhead Mountains mark the Continental Divide. The region not only is surrounded by western lore from the 1860s gold-mining era, but also is home to the Lewis and Clark Trail. Here, Sacajawea recognized the "beaverhead" rock, indicating that she was near her Shoshone tribe's summer homeland. When Meriwether Lewis and his party made contact with the Indians a few days later, the explorers were able to acquire the much-needed horses they required to pursue their trek west.

Later, during the 1877 Nez Perce campaign, a war party following Chief Joseph attacked and killed four ranchers in Horse Prairie Valley. This was in retaliation for the massacre of Nez Perce women and children at the Battle of the Big Hole. Dragging Y history dates to these unsettled times, when tough, yet hopeful pioneers looking for fresh starts did not hesitate to homestead in remote areas of the American West.

A Horse Prairie Perspective

When Roger Peters came to Horse Prairie Valley a century later, he seemed almost as unlucky as those four ranchers. He

Roger Peters and Steve Schroder push some cattle toward the branding pens.

purchased his first ranch in Horse Prairie in 1980, went broke and lost the ranch to the bank six years later.

"That hurt like losing a member of the family," Roger recalled.

He managed, however, to lease back the ranch and made money the following two years. But he still couldn't manage to buy back his old place.

"In those years we would buy yearlings in the spring and grass them over the summer to sell in the fall, because no bank would loan us enough money to buy a mother cow," Roger explained.

In 1989, the Donovan Ranch at the upper end of Horse Prairie was in foreclosure, and Roger purchased it. This was the first of several parcels to be combined to create the Dragging Y. Only two managers had run the Donovan outfit, each for 30 years. The ranch pastures are a combination of rough foothills, as well as large irrigated meadows, where water and grass are plentiful.

Mr. and Mrs. T. H. Hamilton, immigrants from Scotland, had homesteaded the ranch in 1868. The Hamiltons went from penniless to extremely wealthy in 30 years.

In the early 1880s, gold had been discovered in a creek about six miles from their ranch. A camp was established, and soon 10,000 people had moved to the area. The

As is often the case, the ranch brand is used to identify more than cattle and horses.

Hamiltons started milking cows to provide dairy products to the mining camp. The couple dug a large spring-fed pond, which, during the winter, provided ice for the icehouse, where they kept milk, butter and cream at cool temperatures during the summer.

By 1898, the Hamiltons had made enough money to build a large, three-story house. Craftsmen from Europe lived there for two years while working on the house, and all building supplies were hauled to the site with teams and wagons. The Hamiltons made upstairs living quarters for servants, who came and went by an outside staircase.

Sorting cattle before the branding begins is routine work for Jason Ward.

The cowboys keep an eye on the herd, which is turned loose once the branding is complete.

"I won't ask a cowboy to irrigate or put up hay," Roger Peters said. *"Our cowboys spend their time horseback, using the traditional cowboy skills.*

The house boasted intricate hardwood floors made of seven types of wood, as well as beautiful fireplaces with hand-carved wooden mantels. Proud of the horses they raised, the Hamiltons also organized matched races to Dillon, Mont., with their neighbors.

When both the Hamiltons died in approximately 1914, the ranch was sold to Drs. Donovan and Morse, whose wives were sisters. At that time, train track was laid, and the ranch became a railway station, with a post office in the brick house, and a store. Although the tracks eventually were pulled in 1939, "Donovan" still is indicated on some maps as if it were a town.

The bordering LC Ranch came up for sale in 1993, and Roger bought it from Floyd Skelton to add low-elevation winter country to the Dragging Y's high-elevation summer range. Originally named the CL, the LC was homesteaded in 1863 by the Metlen family. When Skelton had purchased the ranch in 1948, he changed the name to LC and owned it for the next 45 years, running mostly yearlings on the outfit.

The same year Roger purchased the LC, the Peters family's home burned to the ground. Roger's wife and children barely escaped the blaze caused by a malfunctioning wood stove.

As a result, Roger casually stated, "Our family history starts in 1993."

In 2001, after leasing it for five years, Roger acquired the Sage Creek Ranch, bringing the Dragging Y to a total of 200,000 acres, a combination of 60,000 deeded acres and leased Bureau of Land Management and national forest land.

"This ranch had good, strong grass," Roger said of Sage Creek.

Sage Creek Ranch was homesteaded in the 1880s by W.K. Knox, but traces its roots to the state's earliest history. In the mid-1860s, as the California Gold Rush reached high gear, two California pioneers drove the first cattle herd into the area of present-day Dillon. They had planned on migrating behind the miners, supplying food along the way, but a bad storm led the pioneers to turn their cattle loose and leave. When they returned a year later, they found the cattle fat and happy, and they decided to stay. Thus began southwestern Montana's cattle industry.

Steve Shroder keeps an eye on the herd during the fall roundup.

Other old homesteads, such as the Brundage, Smith and Salmon places, now part of the Dragging Y, dot Horse Prairie Valley. In the 1910s Salmon had served meals to Gilmore and Pittsburg train crews and passengers. Known as the G & P Train, the outfit was nicknamed the Get Out and Push Train. Nearby Horse Prairie Creek also was nicknamed the Nip and Tuck Creek, so-called for the team of horses that did much work for the railroad at the time.

A Man of Tradition

From the way he tends cattle to the music he prefers, including Ian Tyson and Mike Beck cowboy songs and country tunes, Roger Peters is a man of tradition. For example, because it takes such a long time to pair up cows before loading them in trucks, Dragging Y cattle are trailed from one place to the next only by cowboys horseback.

"Our cows don't get any diesel supplement," Roger joked. "And I think working large numbers of cattle using a horse is extremely efficient and more cost-effective."

All the fences around the ranch are traditional jack-type fences made of lodge poles, and many gates hang from cross-braced jacks. Actually, wire fence rarely is used in mountain valley ranches, since the wire cannot withstand heavy snow loads.

Roger is equally traditional when it comes to the work his cow hands do to earn their wages. He explained, "I won't ask a cowboy to irrigate or put up hay. I hire good cowboys, who spend their time horseback using the traditional cowboy skills."

There never is a lazy day on the Dragging Y. In fact, the first thing Roger might say when interviewing a cowboy job applicant is: "We've got a lot of work."

Foreman Steve Schroder, who used to work for the nearby Matador Cattle Company and then the LC Ranch, has been riding for the Dragging Y brand for 14 years, ever since Roger bought the LC in 1993. In this line of work, where burnout and turnover sometimes are quite high, that is a good sign.

"Schroder came with the LC," Roger joked.

The 3- and 4-year-olds let off a little steam on a brisk morning.

Bloodlines on many of the ranch mares go back to Leo Hancock.

The Foundation Mares

The Draggin Y has been raising horses for some 30 years.

"In 1977, we couldn't get a loan from the bank to buy cattle, so we took some other people's cattle in on a grass lease," Roger recalled. "A fellow by the name of Carl Holt came by and said he had 25 mares he needed to pasture. I said I would be interested because I had been wondering how it would work to run mares on this place, so Carl brought down his mares."

The next day Roger was hanging a gate by the barn when Carl came back to check on his mares. Roger asked how the mares were, and Carl replied, "Oh, just fine. They're all located and look plumb happy. Let me give you a hand on that gate."

Carl helped hang the gate, then came back the next day. And he helped Roger for the next 20 years. A typical "retired" cowboy, Carl couldn't stand not to saddle a horse in the morning and prowl among cattle. He was one of the last old-time cowboys who had grown up horseback, handling a lot of cattle and running wild horses in the Wyoming Red Desert.

Carl always said: "Raise the kind of horses that you like and that work for you, and then find somebody who thinks the way you do to sell them to."

In the late 1940s, Carl had gone to Texas and purchased 10 mares and a stallion, Stormy Weather, out of Lucky Strike. After Stormy Weather was retired, Carl went to Oklahoma to purchase the stallion Leo Hancock, who was Leo on top and Hancock-bred on the bottom. Leo Hancock had been an old-time matched-race horse, the type that used to be taken from town to town to race against the locals' fastest horses. When Leo Hancock became too old for breeding, Carl bought the stallion Kansas Badger, but never had purchased any any outside mares. In 1977, Roger purchased all of Carl's mares

"We're real proud of having the only band of foundation-bred Quarter Horses I know about in this area," Roger said. "These horses are big and rugged, tough and muscular. They've got amiable dispositions, and they're really cowy."

Unfortunately, Carl Holt later fell into a well hidden by old planks and was badly hurt.

The mares and foals browse through the snow on a crisp Montana day.

Sometimes foreman Steve Shroder's day does not go exactly as planned.

Unable to ride any longer, he rapidly went downhill and passed away five years later.

Wearing the Brand

Each November ranch colts are branded in the traditional way, by roping them from horseback. While Roger tends to the branding irons, three cowboys enter an adjacent corral where a band of mares and their foals have been gathered. The cowboys separate a mare-and-colt pair and push the pair into the branding corral.

First, the young horse's photo is taken to be sent to the American Quarter Horse Association, indicating the markings for the registration papers.

Positioned along the fence, foreman Steve Schroder is then ready to work. A colt tries to seek shelter alongside his mother, but it is too late. Two quick twirls and the loop, released by an expert hand, is already on its way, settling accurately around the young horse's neck as another rider escorts the mare from the corral.

This is the colt's first contact with a rope. After a few bounces, he eventually settles down and braces himself against the rope. This is the moment that Roger waits for, to apply the brand on the left shoulder. The branding is also the first step in the weaning process, and the colt is then led to a pasture where he starts his new life.

Sometimes, when a colt doesn't settle down after being roped by the neck, another rider ropes the hind legs to lay him on the ground. A third cowboy then slips off the neck rope, placing it around the front feet, stretching the colt on the ground for branding. Quickly released from the ground, the foal is then led to pasture, where he is turned loose to join his companions.

By day's end the Dragging Y cowboys have branded the newest colt crop. Eventually, the youngsters will become part of the ranch remuda, joining 200 head of Dragging Y horses, among them 48 broodmares and two stallions.

John and Ellen Ward head out to gather the mares and foals.

Mares are pasture-bred, and their foals, born in the open, are raised in that same rough, steep country, an ideal combination that makes them sure-footed and builds stamina. The ranch keeps all the colts, halter-breaking them in the winter after they have been weaned at 6 or 7 months old. The colts are gelded between 18 and 24 months. At age 3, one or two experienced handlers start the colts during the winter, putting 30 days on the youngsters, then leaving them alone until the following summer when their training continues.

As with most big outfits, the Dragging Y cowboys don't ride mares, but do ride the fillies to assess their abilities and dispositions. The horses are then sold as started fillies or put into the broodmare band.

Currently the Dragging Y is home to two stallions. One is Rimfire Lad, a 2000 Quarter Horse by AB Smart Little Mick and out of Doc O Lilly. The other is GCR Okies Lightening, a 2003 Quarter Horse stallion by Okie Super Star and out of Lacey Gambler. Crossing such horses on the ranch mares has proven successful at the Dragging Y.

"These big-boned, tough, gray Leo- and Hancock-bred horses work well for us," Roger said. "We ride over rough and steep terrain, making circles of 35 miles a day, so we need strong horses with good feet, that can handle the job."

Cow horses in this country are experienced in traveling across swift creeks, through deep snow and up and down steep mountain slopes. Because the country is so rough, Dragging Y horses are shod 365 days a year—even in winter, when their regular shoes are replaced by shoes suitable for snow.

Horse-Related Goals

"The cow boss has to be better than all the other cowboys to earn supreme respect," Roger explained.

Cow boss John Ward is responsible for all horse-related business on the Dragging Y Cattle Company. A top hand, he sets a good example for the other cowboys. The Idaho native was influenced early on by the centuries-old ways of the California vaqueros and embraces their tradition of finesse and superior horsemanship. He plans to keep the best horses to become bridle horses, and eventually sell them as "straight up in the bridle."

However, according to John, when it comes to horse training, there is always room for

Ellen Ward can rope with the best of them.

improvement. "If you're satisfied, you're not progressing," he commented.

Lately John and his twin brother, Jason, plus anybody who wants, start an average of 20 colts a year, using the resistance-free style of horsemanship. John likes those who are starting colts to have a feel for a horse, to *ask* a horse to perform, rather than *make* him do things, and to always use a quiet and gentle hand.

Each Dragging Y cowboy can bring three to four personal mounts with him, but, in addition, is issued a string of horses that remain under his authority until the day they are turned back to the ranch. That number varies from person to person, depending on an individual's level of

The Donovan Ranch, part of the Dragging Y, was homesteaded in 1868, and European craftsmen built the three-story brick house in 1898.

experience and on how much he can trust his personal mounts for working cattle. In return, the cowboy must care for his horses, try to further their training, capitalize on the horses' natural abilities and return them in better shape mentally and physically than the day the horses were issued to him. The cowboys ride the horses for four or five years before selling some of them, most when they are 7 to 11 years old.

"Every horse we sell was born on the ranch," Roger said. "We sell the older horses because we have young ones that need riding, so they can receive the same education their older brothers got. We like to sell older, finished, gentle horses that are more desirable because more people can get along with them. When we sell those horses, they have learned everything that can be done horseback and have learned to do it right."

Fueled by the growing interest in ranch rodeos and ranch-horse competitions, which display the skills of the working cowboy and ranch-raised horses, the current demand for seasoned ranch horses continues to be strong and steady.

Lately John's goal has been to sell more horses for performance in the arena. "It's an easy transition for them because they have already done everything outside as ranch horses," he explained.

Obviously, the Dragging Y cowboys take great pride in what these ranch horses can do, and pride is the cowboys' primary motivation.

"Cowboys are the elite of the work force," Roger stated. "They like challenge. For them, there is nothing better than riding good horses they raised and trained themselves."

An old log barn dating back to the early 1900s was remodeled and converted into the ranch office.

Dragging Y Cattle

The Dragging Y runs about 6,200 Black Angus-Charolais-cross cows, and every May leases approximately 270 Charolais bulls to run with the cows until Sept. 1. Roger likes the Charolais breed for its growth ability, and Angus provide the high quality of beef. He also buys bred cows and sells the open cows in the fall.

Calving takes place on the range in April. In early May the cattle go back to the mountains, where they stay until December. During the summer riders check the mountain herds and pack in salt blocks to areas where they want the cattle to congregate. Typically, calves are weaned in the fall and shipped in early December. However, their actual sale occurs during the summer using Superior Livestock's video system.

Because of the Dragging Y's large numbers of cattle, branding takes place throughout the summer, 300 to 400 calves at a time. The sun is still low on the horizon when cowboys fan out to gather a pasture and push the herd toward the branding corral. Cowboys then light the fire and heat the irons.

To avoid unnecessary stress on his stock, Roger opts not to wean the calves.

This crew knows how to stay put and wait for instructions.

"Keeping the cows around has a calming effect on calves and, therefore, they are easier to handle during branding," he explained. "Besides, why separate them for branding when we try to keep them together the rest of the time?"

Two ropers heel and drag calves toward a Nord Fork, a device which the ground crew drops over the calf's neck. This allows them to perform their duties safely and effectively, while saving their energy. Calves are branded, vaccinated and dehorned, and bull calves are

The Dragging Y entrance has a traditional lodgepole jack fence.

Life is good when you can catch some rays on a beautiful fall morning.

castrated. Larger calves are headed and heeled, with the header expertly manipulating his slack to set the animal's position for the heeler. The calf is then stretched and secured between the two ropers without any stress.

Life's Little Pleasures

One of Roger's greatest pleasures in life is working with his family. Another is enjoying the camaraderie of his cowboy crew.

"Raising kids around livestock is a great way to teach them responsibility and compassion. I would rather have my kids helping me than most adults I know," he commented, then advised, "Even if it takes a little longer, take your kids with you."

A demanding but fair boss, Roger also enjoys playing practical jokes on his crew, especially on April Fool's day. One memorable time, he told the cowboys that a Chicago casting agent was in town looking for the next Marlboro Man, and that every cowboy interested in such an opportunity should meet with him for breakfast at 8:00 a.m. at a Dillon restaurant.

Needless to say, several hopeful cowboys showed up at the restaurant, dressed in their best duds, and waited for the casting agent ... and waited. An hour or so later, a friend of

The Dragging Y has an ample supply of branding irons.

Roger's showed up, innocently asking what they were doing there all "duded up." After one cowboy explained, Roger's friend, with a grin, asked if they knew which day it was. That's when the cowboys realized that they'd been had.

Even though Roger enjoys such fun, he also takes his philosophy about ranching seriously. He explained, "Although ranching is a great life to raise a family, loving horses or even cattle is not a good enough reason to become a rancher. You have to love the land. Ranching is about having a relationship with the land. You have to nurture it, listen to it, be patient with it and forgive it. If you do, the land will give back to you."

Dragging Y Timeline

1860s: Texas cattle were first trailed north to Montana.

1863: The LC Ranch, which became part of the Dragging Y, was homesteaded.

1868: The Donovan Ranch, now also part of the Dragging Y, was homesteaded.

1877: Four Horse Prairie Valley ranchers died in a Nez Perce attack.

1940s: Carl Holt traveled to Texas to purchase 10 mares and Stormy Weather, developing the bloodlines that were to later influence the Dragging Y remuda.

1949: Leo Hancock was born. This stallion, which Carl Holt later purchased, also greatly influenced Dragging Y Cattle Company horses.

1973: Roger and Carrie Peters moved from Colorado to Montana.

1977: Carl Holt pastured 25 mares on Roger Peters' place, and the mares became seed stock for the Dragging Y broodmare band.

1989: Roger Peters purchased the Donovan Ranch.

1993: The LC Ranch, adjoining the Donovan, was purchased to become part of the Dragging Y, and the Peters family home burned to the ground.

2001: Roger Peters purchased Sage Creek Ranch, which he had leased for the prior five years, increasing the Dragging Y's territory to 200,000 acres.

2006: Roger Peters purchased the Harkness Ranch in Big Sheep Basin.

*"If you don't have
a horse in every pasture,
you really aren't ranching."
Walt Haythorn*

5

HAYTHORN LAND AND CATTLE CO.

By Guy de Galard

Haythorn Land and Cattle Company is known as one of the great American ranches, as well as one of the last bastions of cowboy tradition, where horse-drawn, wooden-wheeled wagons still are used during the spring roundup. Located north of Ogallala, Neb., the legendary 65,000-acre outfit's horse program earned the American Quarter Horse Association's inaugural Best Remuda Award in 1992.

From England to Ogallala

The Haythorn Ranch story began in Lancaster, England, in 1876, when 16-year-old Harry Haythornthwaite, heartbroken because he was not allowed to marry his sweetheart, stowed

Few outfits in the country rely on horses as much as Haythorn Land and Cattle Company.

Craig Haythorn, who currently runs the outfit, credits his father, Waldo, for building the ranch into what it is today.

Once in Ogallala, Harry opened a livery barn, shortened his name to Haythorn and married a local girl, Emma Gilpin. Harry eventually sold the livery barn and went to work as a wagon boss for a man named Yeast near Arthur, Neb., and took payment for his wages in cattle, at $10 a head. Emma helped, as well, by cooking for the cowhands. Each time she served more than 10 men at the table, she was paid 25 cents.

The couple saved every penny they made and in 1884 filed on a land-grant section four miles east of Arthur. Leading a packhorse, Emma routinely rode sidesaddle to Ogallala, 40 miles away, to buy the supplies they needed. Little by little, the couple began putting together what is known today as one of the premier ranching operations in the country. As they did, the Haythorn family helped transform the Sand Hills into what they are today—cowboy country.

The Aquifer, Dunes and Die-Ups

The Sand Hills area is the largest grass-stabilized dune region in the world, and underneath an ocean of gramma, bluestem and buffalo grass, which help hold down the sand, lies the continent's largest water source—the Ogallala Aquifer. Thanks to this natural underground reservoir, the Sand Hills seldom suffer from drought.

The first explorers traveling through the Sand Hills country called it a "great desert of drifting sand," but the Sioux Indians, who had hunted buffalo in this area for centuries, knew better. And so did Harry.

While settling in the area in the 1880s, he saw this 20,000-square-mile sea of grass-covered sand dunes as prime cattle and horse country. The soft, sandy soil does not require that horses be shod. Locals often say: "If you find a rock around here, it was brought from somewhere else."

Nonetheless, loose and dry sand can be as treacherous for vehicles as deep mud. As opposed to regular dirt, which can become a quagmire when wet, the Sand Hills actually are easier to travel after a good rain has packed the sand, rather than when the sand is dry.

But the Nebraska winters can be brutal, and heavy snowfall can create snowdrifts as high as the 20-foot windmills dotting the landscape. One of the toughest winters to withstand, the "Big Die-Up" of 1885-'86, almost wiped out Harry and Emma's newly established ranch.

away on a ship bound for America. When his unauthorized presence was discovered, the ship already was six days out to sea. The captain, however, took a liking to the boy and put him to work to earn his passage, directing young Harry to care for a load of Hereford bulls being shipped to Texas. Having grown up on a farm, Harry was no stranger to livestock. He did his job well and, on his arrival in Galveston, was hired by the rancher who had purchased the bulls.

During the next eight years, Harry worked as a cowhand and made four drives up the Old Texas Trail, two into Kansas and two to Nebraska, specifically Ogallala. When the Union Pacific Railroad line had reached Ogallala in 1866, the town made its name in the cattle business as "The End of the Old Texas Trail." Following Harry's final drive to Ogallala, he decided to stay, and by 1884 the last great cattle drives from Texas north on Nebraska's Western Trail had come to an end.

During another severe winter in 1913, the couple lost 800 head of cattle.

Walt, Harry's son, described that blizzard and its horrible results: "It was March 13, 1913. The day began with a cold rain, and our stock was soaked. That night, it started to snow and blow, and the thermometer hit 25 degrees below zero. It howled around here for three days so hard you couldn't see five feet. Fifty-foot drifts piled up in the gulleys and pockets, literally smothering hundreds of critters. Some of them had ice and snow as big as washtubs balled around their heads when we found them. It hit us at calving time and I remember the hands picking up dead beef critters in a wagon that held 54 bodies. Every time they went out they filled the wagon, and they went out a lot."

A 1931 blizzard was equally devastating for Walt and his family. A good portion of the cattle froze to death in their tracks, and the storm proved almost fatal to Walt. He followed a fence line, post by post and gate to gate, for several miles in blinding snow, until he came to a familiar gate, which helped him find his way home. At the time, it took him more than 90 minutes to travel less than a mile. Starving colts in a winter pasture had eaten all the hair off their dead companions and chewed the manes and tails off each other.

More recently, Craig, Harry's great-grandson and the current ranch owner, experienced winter hardship during a 1975 blizzard. It claimed the lives of 750 calves.

But as Walt once said philosophically: "It could have been worse, it could have killed the cows."

The Haythorn Legacy

Through the years, Walt Haythorn and his son, Waldo, Craig's grandfather and father respectively, became the true architects of the ranch's Quarter Horse program. Walt was known to say, "If you don't have a horse in every pasture, you really aren't ranching."

Born Aug. 9, 1893, Walt, and his younger brother, Harry, spent summers on the ranch, learning the cowboy trade by working hard alongside their father, Harry Sr. One summer, as teenagers, the boys had jobs counting cattle on government land. Harry Sr., thinking that his boys had too much free time on their hands, gave them a few colts to start. To break the colts to lead, the brothers haltered

Much like his father and grandfather, Sage Haythorn, Craig's son, has strong interests in both ranching and rodeo.

two horses, tied them together with the leads through the corral fence and let each jerk the other back and forth until the horses were ready to lead.

Whatever Walt took an interest in, he gave everything he had, and he was completely dedicated to ranching. If he left the house for the day, he went prepared for any event that might occur, loading his vehicle with his saddle, bridle, spurs, leggings, windmill box, coat, gloves, cap and more.

Waldo was born to Walt and wife Hazel in 1917. By the time Waldo was 16, he already was running the summer hay crew, and he officially began to run the ranch when he became a married man. Waldo was as carefree as Walt was intense. A hard worker, Waldo also loved people and had a great sense of humor.

"My dad could walk into a room with 200 people and, within five minutes, he'd have them all laughing," Craig recalled of his father. "He was known nationwide."

by crossing the Thoroughbred stallions with mares from his herd of 500. Horses, Harry figured, would pay the ranch expenses, and cattle would provide the money to buy more land. Now, horses pay for most of the overhead.

The ranch did not get its first Quarter Horse until after Harry had passed away. The Haythorn Ranch bought a load of bred mares from the Waggoner Ranch in Vernon, Texas, in the 1930s, and later an Oklahoma stallion, Sport, arrived at Haythorn Land and Cattle Company. He became Nebraska's first registered Quarter Horse, as well as grand champion at the National Western Stock Show in Denver.

Influential Haythorn Stallions

In 1951, Walt purchased Eddie, a 1940 sorrel stallion, who became a cornerstone of the Haythorn horse-breeding program. Eddie was sired by the famed Thoroughbred stallion Raffles, and out of a grade mare, Greta 1, by Bonnie Jack. Eddie possessed first-rate cow sense, and his offspring, which included 154 registered foals, proved to be very athletic. In 1958, Eddie 40, by Eddie and out of Sports

Roan, a daughter of Sport, was born and subsequently raised on the ranch, thus continuing the Eddie foundation in the Haythorn horses' bloodlines.

The Haythorns also owned My Beaver, by Jess Hankins' Beaver Creek and out of FL Pee Wee, by Peter McCue Jr. A 1958 sorrel stallion, My Beaver sired 141 registered foals, nine of which earned a total of 1,111.5 AQHA points and an AQHA Championship.

Later the Haythorns started adding Hancock and Driftwood bloodlines to the mix. In 1977, Eddie Eighty, sired by Eddie 40 and out of Tootie Toot 71, by Buck Hancock, was foaled on the ranch. Although the ranch lost him at only 15 years of age, the stallion was an outstanding influence on the Haythorn horse program.

"He was one of the best horses we ever raised," Craig commented.

Through the years, the ranch horse program has worked. Haythorn Land and Cattle Company won the inaugural AQHA-Bayer Animal Health Best Remuda Award in 1992, which Waldo accepted at the 1993 National Cattlemen's Association Convention in

According to Craig Haythorn, there is no substitute for the daily ranch activities the outfit's horses experience.

Phoenix. In 2001, the year before Waldo passed away, he was inducted in the American Quarter Horse Hall of Fame.

The Haythorns have continued to upgrade their horses ever since, and today the ranch, recognized worldwide, is one of the largest producers of American Quarter Horses in the United States. Now the stallion roster includes horses whose bloodlines trace closely to Colonel Freckles, Doc O'Lena, Docs Hickory, King Fritz, Nu Cash, Playgun and Tanquery Gin.

Breeding Haythorn Horses

Today, horses continue to play significant roles in the Haythorn Ranch's ongoing success. The ranch breeds for big, athletic, flat-boned, well-balanced horses that have stamina, sound feet and well-formed withers. Weighing between 1,200 and 1,300 pounds at maturity, the ranch horses can handle long riding days.

Craig Haythorn's primary goal is to raise quality Quarter Horses that excel on the ranch, as well as in the arena.

"You have to be able to work a horse daily on a real ranch to have a true ranch horse. There is no substitute for the day-to-day ranch activities that make an excellent ranch horse," Craig stated, adding that the ranch also has made it a priority to breed horses for willing dispositions. "In other words," Craig said, "capable horses that are more user-friendly."

Through the years, Craig has developed an almost photographic memory for horse pedigrees and bloodlines. Every fall, he sits down and studies pedigrees, considering which stallions have worked well and on which bands of mares. Many mares have been at the ranch for years and consistently have produced supreme foals by the same stallions.

"I have a pretty good idea of what works," Craig said. "I may switch some mares around, among the different broodmare bands, and experiment until I get them all just right. If a certain cross doesn't [seem right], I just try something different the following year."

All horses on the ranch are pasture-bred. Each spring, the ranch's 150 broodmares are divided into several bands and turned out with stallions until the end of July. Among the ranch's 14 stallions are two grandsons of King Fritz and one son of Playgun, PG Shogun, out of Miss Sho Bunny by Shogun San. PG Shogun's

Tradition holds at the Haythorn; Craig is the only man in the pen roping horses, and, yes, he's throwing a left-handed loop.

awards include being named the 2004 Western Heritage Classic Champion Ranch Horse in the open division and Working Ranch Cowboys Association 2006 open-division and reining champion.

Although the ranch always has featured a wide palette of horse colors, the Haythorns do not try to breed for a specific color. As Waldo often said: "A good horse is never a bad color."

Draft-Horse Hitches

In addition to raising Quarter Horses, the ranch also maintains 45 head of Belgian-Percheron draft horses, and several work mares foal each spring. The drafts are used in six-horse hitches to pull the feed wagon during the winter, and the horses stack more than 6,000 tons of hay each summer. Teams also pull the wagons during the spring roundup. Both Craig and Haythorn horseman Mark Goodman are expert at driving teams, and they enjoy it.

"It's more fun doing things the old way," Mark admitted.

But to this day, the ranch's affinity for draft horses has less to do with nostalgia than with economic reasons. Craig explained, "I've never had a draft horse that wouldn't start in the morning."

Haythorn Horse Training

Ranch colts and fillies are halter-broken between 1 and 2 months old, branded at the end of July and weaned around Oct. 1 each year. Colts are gelded the following April.

Young horses are started under saddle as 2-year-olds and handled for 30 days before being turned loose for three or four months. Then the youngsters join the remuda, where their training continues by being ridden on small circles. In other words, the youngsters are used when a cowboy checks not-too-distant cattle; mature horses make the big circles, which usually involve longer hours and greater distances. In time, the young horses are ridden on increasingly larger circles to check cattle and also become familiar with roping, even dragging a few calves for the experience. By age 4, the young horses are expected to earn their keep by gathering pastures, dragging calves to the branding fire and sorting cattle.

Each Haythorn cowboy has a string of 10 to 15 horses, including two or three colts. It is the cowboy's responsibility to put the finishing

Haythorn cowboys moving the remuda stop for a water break.

Jesse Hefner waters his horse by one of the numerous windmills that dot the Sand Hills.

touches on the young horses put in his care, and when his mounts are sold, he collects 10 percent of the sale price.

Veteran cowboy Mark Goodman has quite an extensive background in handling horses. However, his outlook on starting and training horses has changed significantly the past several years, since he was first exposed to a more gentle approach. Each year, Haythorn cowboys are given the opportunity to attend colt-starting clinics conducted by such renowned horsemen and clinicians as Buck Brannaman, Buster McLaury, Bryan Neubert and Joe Wolter.

"There is a difference between conquering a horse and making him a willing partner," the seasoned cowboy said. "Both ways work, but if the horse *wants* to do what he is asked to do, you get a better end-result. If I had known then what I know now, the horses I've trained would have been much better."

Haythorn Horse Sales

The first Haythorn Land and Cattle Company Production Sale was held in 1979 and was well-attended. The Haythorn family offered 75 Quarter Horses, 42 draft horses and six mules, as well as 80 Longhorns and 150 commercial Hereford heifers. The next sale took place in 1984, when the ranch celebrated its 100th anniversary, and more than 4,000 people nationwide came, breaking attendance records.

In 1995, the Haythorns built the Figure Four Traditions Event Center, which originally was designated to house activities accompanying the large horse sales. Today, the 7,200 square-foot rental facility is available to host a wide variety of events, from small family reunions to large venues, such as the Nebraska Cattlemen's Ball. Open year-round, the facility often is booked a year in advance.

Initially held every four years in early September, a Haythorn sale has been an annual event since 2000. The ranch typically offers between 100 and 250 horses for sale, including an extensive selection of seasoned ranch geldings, to buyers coming from all over the world., The 2006 production sale offered more than 500 horses for viewing, the largest selection of Haythorn horses to be offered at one time. An added bonus: Beginning in 2003, any horse purchased at the ranch production sale became eligible to compete in the Waldo Haythorn Reining Futurity, created to honor Craig's father.

Family patriarch Waldo Haythorn often said, "A good horse is never a bad color."

The Haythorn is recognized worldwide as one of the top Quarter Horse producers in the United States.

89

"We sell [horses] mostly for ranch use or roping," Craig stated. "Because we breed and raise the horses we sell, we feel it's an absolute necessity to stand behind our product."

Haythorn Cattle

Although the ranch is known mostly for its horse program, cattle continue to play an important role. But, as Waldo Haythorn often explained, "The only reason we have cows on this place is to make good horses."

Today, the Haythorns run Angus cows crossed on black bulls, and black white-faced cows that are crossed with Charolais bulls. The cattle are stocked at about 50 cow-calf pairs to the section for six months of the year. Cows calve in the open during March and April. The Haythorn calves, known for their uniformity and breeding, very often top the fall sales.

Cattle are sold via video broadcasting, which has broadened the livestock market by reaching potential buyers worldwide. Craig commented that such video sales marketing "has been very well-received."

A sense of nostalgia keeps a small herd of Longhorns on the Haythorn. In 1969, Craig became interested in Longhorn cattle and bought seven bulls and three pure-bred heifers. He also bought some foundation cows from the YO Ranch in Mountain Home, Texas. For many years following, the family built a quality herd, winning several awards for champion Longhorn steers and cows throughout the region. These Haythorn Longhorns also have been admired for their fertility and winter survival skills.

Living on the Wagon

Haythorn Land and Cattle Company is one of the finest in holding with true Western ranching traditions, and the family takes great pride in preserving the rich heritage of the ranch's founding father.

All Haythorn cowboys appreciate the old-fashioned ways of doing things, such as riding and roping, but they consider spring branding and living on the wagon their favorite time of all. After calving in the cold and mending fences, the cowboys look forward to riding herd

In a scene right out of the Old West, the Haythorn wagon and remuda head cross-country to the next camp.

on the remuda and heading for the first camp. The chuck wagon, bed wagon and water supply follow, bumping across the rolling grasslands.

"Living out on the wagon during branding and camping out during these three weeks is an exciting time for all of us, and we are sorry to see it end," Craig commented. "Going out with the wagons also saves time. We don't have to worry about being back at a certain time and driving back and forth between the ranch and the branding sites. It's just a more relaxed atmosphere."

Every morning at camp, in the predawn chill, two cowboys head out at a trot to jingle the remuda of 150 geldings and drive them into a rope corral. There, Craig, who, according to tradition, is the only man in the corral, ropes each mount with a quick, graceful and accurate left-handed houlihan throw. As each cowboy calls out the name of the horse he intends to ride that day, Craig ropes and leads the horse to his rider, who slips on his bridle.

It is not uncommon for younger, frisky ranch horses to have cold backs in the

The Haythorn is one of the few remaining outfits that still use horse-drawn, wooden-wheeled wagons during branding.

According to Waldo Haythorn, cattle "make good horses," a view shared by Haythorns through the years.

Jake Stutzman and J.C. Piepho team up to flank a calf.

morning and throw a few bucks when their riders mount. Most cowboys, especially the younger ones, view such as a fun challenge and just ride through the situation. At the Haythorn, however, most cowboys first work from the ground and make a point of warming up their mounts, "gypping" their horses at a trot in small circles, before ever stepping into their stirrups. Once everyone is saddled, the cowboys strike out at a trot to make the circle and gather cattle for the morning's branding.

At the branding site, irons are heated with a wood fire, another ranch tradition. The horses not used for roping are hobbled, a necessity in this treeless country. Once the cow herd has been penned in the large, open-ended corral, four riders rope and drag calves to the fire while the rest of the crew wrestles, castrates, dehorns and vaccinates the young cattle.

Craig, iron in hand, walks from one calf to the next to apply the ranch's trademark "Figure Four" brand. Everything is done smoothly and efficiently. The air is filled with smoke and the anxious bawling of cattle. Dust sticks to the men's sweaty faces, and their muscles grow tired as they flank calves. The

crew brands about 300 calves a day, typically half in the morning and the remainder during the afternoon.

The crew remains camped for a few days, until every calf they can find on that part of the ranch has been branded. Then, it is time to break camp. The food is stacked away in the chuck wagon, and the bedrolls loaded on another wagon. Craig, driving the chuck wagon leads the way to the next camp, followed by the remuda, strung out and flanked by the cowboys. The squeaky wheels of the wagons and horses' whinnies add sound to this scene from a different time.

However, not everything always goes smoothly when the crew is out with the wagon—like the night a hailstorm destroyed the cook tent, putting a big tear through the middle of it. Undeterred, the camp crew managed to resurrect the tent. Soon hot coffee was poured, and a hearty breakfast cooked in a Dutch oven.

"I've always just loved cowboy life and the Western atmosphere. The wagon still works for us, and I am trying to keep all this alive," said Craig, who first went out with the spring wagon when he was 4 years old.

The Haythorn cowboys water their horses following an afternoon of branding.

Rodeo: A Haythorn Tradition

Although best known for their horse and ranching operations, the Haythorn family has been deeply involved in rodeo for generations. Even today, the ranch still raises bucking bulls that are sold at private treaty.

Competitive events give Haythorn horsemen opportunities to showcase the outfit's stallions and working ranch geldings.

Years ago, Walt and Harry Haythorn Jr., helped to pioneer the sport in Nebraska. Walt participated in the first Ogallala Roundup in 1916, rode saddle broncs, wrestled steers, competed in steer roping and calf roping, and eventually produced rodeos.

Later, Waldo and his cousin, Howard, traveled the rodeo circuit for years, dominating roping, as well as cutting events, across the country. The Haythorn cousins often were on the winners list at such major rodeos as the Pendleton (Ore.) Roundup and Cheyenne (Wyo.) Frontier Days. Waldo was a charter member of the old Cowboys Turtle Association, the forerunner of the Rodeo Cowboys Association, which later became the Professional Rodeo Cowboys Association.

Craig rodeoed through high school, was state champion four consecutive years in calf roping and cutting, and took two National High School Rodeo titles in cutting. A good portion of his college tuition was paid with money he won while rodeoing. For 20 years he held a PRCA card and competed in

The sign proclaims the importance of savvy horsemanship on the Haythorn.

calf roping, team roping, steer roping and bulldogging.

In 1988, Haythorn Land and Cattle Company ranch was invited to compete in the 4th Annual Western Heritage Classic Ranch Rodeo in Abilene, Texas.

"Although we were the only out-of-state ranch to be invited, we were fortunate enough to win the overall high-point award," said Craig. Since then, the ranch has won the same honor five more times and has tied with the Four Sixes Ranch for having won the championship the most times. Today, ranch horse competitions and ranch rodeos provide additional avenues for the Haythorns to promote their horses.

"We started going to ranch rodeos just because we loved to compete," Craig said, "but we came to realize that it was an excellent opportunity for us to showcase our young breeding stallions and our working ranch geldings. This way, we can give people from all over the country a firsthand look at what we have."

The Haythorn sons, Cord and Sage, are the fifth Haythorn generation to be connected with the ranch, and they, as well as daughter Shaley, seem to be following Craig's footsteps into the rodeo arena. Craig, Cord, Sage and Shaley all have won rookie-of-the-year awards in the Nebraska High School Rodeo Association. The two brothers, highly competitive throughout high school and college, have won numerous awards at the state and national level in calf roping and team roping.

Although both brothers help during branding, Sage developed a keen interest in ranching. He currently studies the equine industry at West Texas A&M University in Canyon, Texas, where he continues to compete in the college rodeo circuit. Cord has completed auctioneer training and, when time allows, enjoys helping his uncles at the Torrington (Wyo.) Livestock Sale facilities.

Contrary to tradition on most large ranches, the Haythorn doesn't have a cowboss per se. Craig and his father, Waldo, ran the ranch together until 1989, when Waldo had a stroke and Craig took over management of the entire ranch. Today, Craig wears

Haythorn Land and Cattle Company Timeline

1876: Sixteen years old and heartbroken, Harry Haythornwaite stowed away on a ship bound from England to Galveston, Texas.

1884: Harry and wife Emma filed on a land-grant section 4 miles from Arthur, Neb., to lay the foundations of Haythorn Land and Cattle Company.

1885-'86: The "Big Die-Up," the result of a severe blizzard, almost put the young Haythorns out of the ranching business.

1893: Walt Haythorn was born to Harry and Emma.

1913: The Haythorn lost 800 head of cattle in a blizzard.

1917: Waldo Haythorn, Walt's son and Craig's father, was born.

1931: Another blizzard, in which Walt Haythorn almost died, again resulted in huge cattle losses.

1942: Waldo purchased the Broken Axle.

1946: Walt Haythorn showed the ranch stallion, Sport, to top honors at Denver's National Western Livestock Show and Rodeo.

1949: Waldo purchased the Smith Ranch.

1951: The Haythorn purchased Eddie, a stallion who became one of the cornerstones in the ranch's breeding program.

1975: A winter blizzard killed 750 Haythorn calves, testing both Waldo's and Craig's mettle.

1977: Eddie Eighty, who later became one of the top Haythorn horses, was born.

1979: Haythorn Land and Cattle Company held its first production sale.

1983: Craig Haythorn married Jody Madden on Waldo and wife Bel's 40th anniversary.

1989: Waldo Haythorn purchased the Frye Place and that same year suffered a serious stroke.

1992: Haythorn Land and Cattle Company earned the inaugural Best Remuda Award presented by the American Quarter Horse Association and Bayer Animal Health.

2003: The Waldo Haythorn Reining Futurity was created to honor the family patriarch.

the hats of owner, manager and cowboss. A top hand, he is well-respected by his crew and appreciated for being a man of integrity, true to his word, a man for whom a handshake is worth a written contract.

"I hope one of our sons will be interested in taking over some day, but I am not pushing them," said Craig, who never questioned his own career path. Running the ranch is all he ever wanted to do.

"Chigger certainly tops my list as the smartest and most lovable horse I have ever ridden....He could do everything but talk English."
George Ellis

6

BELL RANCH

By Guy de Galard

It is 6:00 a.m. The breakfast bell echoes through the ranch headquarters. The aroma of bacon and freshly brewed coffee comes from the cook shack and floats through the cool morning air. Pickups pull in, unloading cowboys. A new day has started on the Bell.

Workdays on New Mexico's Bell Ranch began in earnest almost two centuries ago, and since then the ranch has weathered changing fortunes, as well as changing governments. The Spanish first ruled the region, followed by the Mexicans and eventually the Americans. Upon acquisition of the New Mexico Territory, the U.S. Cavalry established a temporary post at Fort Bascom, where the Bell Ranch headquarters stand today.

Huerfano Mountain stands in the background as mares and their foals are gathered prior to weaning.

Colby Gunnels rides for the Bell Ranch brand.

Early Ranch History

The Bell Ranch originated in 1824 with two Spanish land grants, totaling about 700,000 acres of rolling grassland and red rimrocked canyons—the Baca Location Number Two and the vast Pablo Montoya grant, given to a former Spanish army captain by the same name. Comanche, Kiowa and Apache hunted buffalo on the land Montoya received, but pictographs carved in the red cliffs indicate that Native Americans might have lived there before the 1500s.

Although Pablo Montoya's family had been established in Santa Fe for almost 200 years, his dream was different. He envisioned an open land of good grass and flowing water, where he and his family could establish a domain that would endure long after he was gone.

The Comanche, however, posed an immediate problem in the early 1800s. The land had been their hunting grounds, and they responded to this new alien encroachment by running off Montoya's horses and killing his cattle, forcing the family to return to Santa Fe's safety for a brief time. Eventually, Montoya returned to his grant, made peace with the Comanche and became a Comanchero by trading with them and the neighboring Kiowas.

By 1867, however, the Montoya ownership had been extinguished, and his attorney, John S. Watts of Santa Fe, had gained title to the entire grant. Three years later, Watts sold that grant to Wilson Waddingham, a flamboyant Canadian promoter and land speculator, who is credited with registering the Bell brand in 1875 and upgrading the native cows with Durham bulls.

During those days, the New Mexico territory was still rough and often dangerous. The years from 1872 through 1874 saw savage raids carried out by Kiowas and angry Comanche warriors. White rustlers even took advantage of the situation by dressing up as Indians and stealing livestock, most of which Waddingham eventually managed to recover.

In 1876 Waddingham tried to build a new brick headquarters north of La Cinta Creek, a little upstream from the old Montoya buildings, but the new headquarters burned down before Waddingham could move there. Another new headquarters complex grew up nearby, centered around a sprawling adobe residence that would become known—after whitewashing—as the "White House."

In this arid land, far horizons are dotted with mesquite, cedar and yucca. High mesas with Spanish names, such as *Huerfano*, or orphan, and *Gavilan*, the hawk, break the horizon. Legendary cattle baron Charles Goodnight once used the prominent Gavilan mesa as a landmark to help him navigate his way to Colorado with his cattle herds. *Medio*, a tall mesa on the ranch's eastern edge is 1,500 feet higher than the headquarters.

"At Medio one has the feeling of being almost on top of a world that is absolutely empty—a world of distant ridges and faint, far-away rimrocks," Mattie Ellis, wife of longtime manager George Ellis, once said.

La Campana, the bell-shaped mesa, marks the center of the spread and gives the ranch its name and brand.

Wagon boss Carroll Jack Lewis, who believes in strong, versatile horses, is ready to put a ride on 2-year-old Blue Duck.

Further improvements occurred about 1886, when ranch manager Mike Slattery put 140 miles of barbed-wire fence around the Bell range to facilitate branding at roundup time and to contain the livestock. To this day, the Bell Ranch has had a fine reputation for its good fences.

By 1890, Waddingham was in serious financial trouble. From the mid-1880s, range overuse, harsh winters, drought and depressed cattle markets had made the Bell unprofitable. In 1894 control of the company was taken over by John Greenbough and James Brown Potter, two leading New York City financiers, who quickly discharged Mike Slattery. Ever hoping to regain control of the Montoya Grant, Waddingham continued to finance speculative schemes until he died of a heart attack in 1899.

Through the following years, the ranch, which at one time boasted 52,000 head of cattle and 1,000 horses, went through several ownerships and reorganizations. Slattery was replaced by Arthur Tisdall, a friendly Irishman and respected cattleman from Texas, where he had been ranch manager of the JA Ranch in the Palo Duro Canyon. Unfortunately, Tisdall's career was cut short when he died four years later of pneumonia.

Stability, Then Sales

A new era of stability began in 1899 with the coming of E. G. Stoddard, his associates and their Red River Valley Company, based in New Haven, Conn. For the next 49 years, property ownership was vested in this company, which had only two presidents and two general managers during that time. Charles O'Donel, who managed the outfit from 1898 to 1932, is credited with installing the first windmills and telephone lines at the Bell Ranch. Albert K. Mitchell, who was at the helm from 1933 to 1947, became one of the early presidents of the American Quarter Horse Association.

But in 1947 the land was divided into six large parcels, each drawn so that the resulting ranch parcel would have a good supply of water.

"It was a sad day," George Ellis recalled. "It was time to divide up the remuda and for many of the old crew to say goodbye. Right after breakfast, a sleepy, heartsick crew gathered at the horse corral to choose their horses and gather up their gear. One after another, the favorites were called for, roped, and led out. By noon the cream of the Bell remuda was gone. But we still had the mares and the young horses, so in a few years we again had a remuda to be proud of."

Cayce Joe Lewis warms up "Hollywood," a 5-year-old gelding.

The headquarters unit and brand sold to Harriet E. Keeney of Connecticut. This piece, encompassing 130,855 acres, became the Bell Ranch. Keeney hired George Ellis as ranch manager, and he remained at the helm until his retirement in 1970. That same year headquarters buildings were placed on the National Register of Historic Places.

The ranch then sold to the late William Lane, who later added the Waggoner northern division parcel to the Bell.

"The ranch doubled in size overnight," current ranch manager Bert Ancell noted. As a 16-year-old, Bert came to work on the ranch's spring wagon in 1968, and he has been at the Bell ever since.

With the purchase of that northern division, the Lanes hired Don Hofman, who served as manager until his 1986 retirement. He was succeeded by Rusty Tinnin. Following Tinnin's death in 2006, Ancell was promoted from his assistant manager position, which he had held for 27 years.

Today, the ranch encompasses 292,000 acres and is bordered by Conchas Lake on the south and the Canadian river on the northwest side. In addition to the headquarters, the ranch maintains five camps with families, and each "camp man" is responsible for his section of the ranch, managing it as if it were his own. The ranch is now owned by a trust for Bill Lane's five children. One son, Jeff, had raised his family on the Bell until August 15, 2007, when the plane he was piloting on the ranch crashed, and he was killed.

Bell Cattle Innovations

Until 1894, when then-manager Arthur Tisdall purchased the first purebred Herefords from the JA Ranch in Texas, the New Mexico country was stocked with native cattle. Within the first three years, Tisdall had purchased 1,000 Hereford bulls from the JA, thus sparking significant improvement in the quality of Bell Ranch cattle. According to historical records, no other New Mexico ranch used so many Hereford bulls at such an early date.

In 1898, under the guidance of new manager Charles M. O'Donel, the ranch continued to use purebred bulls to improve native cattle and steadily pursued that practice for many years. O'Donel also added Shorthorn bulls to the sire battery, and for many years thereafter it became common practice to use about half Shorthorn bulls and half Herefords on the Bell cows.

Son Cayce Joe and father Carroll Jack Lewis compete together on the outfit's ranch rodeo team.

On weaning day mares and their foals are gathered off the Mule Pasture.

The ranch founded a purebred Shorthorn herd in 1901 when 102 cows were purchased from Albert Harrah, Newton, Iowa. Sires representing prominent bloodlines included six grandsons of the English Royal champion Choice. The ranch then purchased Hereford bulls in sufficient numbers to maintain the balance between herd-sire breeds until 1914, when the ranch established its registered Hereford herd. Missouri cattle breeders Gudgell and Simpson's sire, Beau Brummel, recognized as one of the greatest Hereford bulls, was a determining factor in selecting the first three bulls to become part of the Bell's registered Hereford herd.

O'Donel also inaugurated the practice of selling the ranch's beef output as yearlings, rather than keeping the cattle until they were 4 or 5 years old. For more than three decades, O'Donel implemented previous manager Arthur Tisdall's vision of the Bell Ranch as a cow-calf operation.

However, when Albert Mitchell took over ranch management in the early 1930s, a severe drought yielding less than 25 percent of the region's normal rainfall, as well as the Depression, called for drastic measures. By the fall of 1933, Mitchell had scattered Bell cattle all the way from Southern California to Pennsylvania and into the northern Mexican state of Sonora. In 1935, with the return of more normal moisture conditions, the Bell cow herd increased to more than 10,000 head.

By the mid-1930s, the registered herd, which O'Donel had established as the principal source of bulls for the range cow herd, was badly in need of culling, so Mitchell stopped using Shorthorn bulls to concentrate on horned Hereford bulls. Mitchell also took O'Donel's innovative marketing concept one step further by marketing the ranch's production as weaner calves instead of yearling steers, now the industry standard. According to Mitchell, this marketing program enabled him "to keep up numbers of cows and provide good insurance in dry seasons."

When George Ellis took over as ranch manager in 1947, he inherited all the Bell cattle, which included a herd of purebred Herefords and about 1,700 high-grade range cattle. One of Ellis' innovative ideas was to introduce the concept of beef-production testing, which consisted of weighing calves at 205 days to measure their performance. Documented in the July 1959 *American Hereford Journal*, Ellis' concept has proven successful, and the practice has since become the industry standard. Widely regarded as an industry pioneer, Ellis was named New Mexico Cattleman of the Year in 1952. When Ellis retired in 1970, Don Hofman

Only a few of the Bell Ranch horses are buckskins, bays or other colors; most are sorrels.

The Bell has long been known for its sorrel horses with white markings.

Weanlings typically are separated from their dams in mid-October.

became Bell Ranch manager and remained in charge until his 1986 retirement, when Rusty Tinnin took over.

With Tinnin at the helm, another pioneering concept was born—Red Bell cattle. In 1990, after running purebred Hereford for almost a century, the ranch started developing its own breed. A hardy composite breed of Gelbvieh, Hereford, Red Angus and Brahma breeding, Red Bell cattle are able to withstand year-to-year variations in precipitation and feed availability.

The ranch currently runs 3,000 cows in their primary breeding herds. The Bell also maintains a few Longhorn bulls that are bred to the first-calf heifers for calving ease. Heifers and cows still calve unassisted on open range, and spring branding is done from the wagon.

Bell Ranch Horses

Since the early days, horses have been an important part of the Bell operation, and initial efforts to improve the horse herd included breeding the original stock of Spanish mares with purebred stallions. Arabians were the first used for this purpose, and later some Morgan stallions, as well as Thoroughbreds, were introduced.

In the 1890s, the Bell Ranch mares and young stock were gathered and moved to Mesa Rica, a high tableland located on the ranch's southwestern portion. Ranch hand Jake Muniz moved there to begin breaking the young horses that would soon become part of the Bell remuda.

When O'Donel came to manage the Bell in 1898, many wild horses roamed the ranch. From time to time, some were rounded up from the ridge tops and driven down to the canyon bottoms, where they were mixed with gentler saddle horses. Then, 60 to 75 of the wild horses were roped and herded back to the ranch headquarters, to be broken for future saddle-horse use. Eventually, most of the 1,100 horses running wild on the ranch were gathered and sold for $3.50 a head.

Later, the ranch began using Quarter Horses in the horse program because the breed's disposition and athletic abilities best met ranch work demands. By the 1930s, Albert Mitchell had made it a point to raise capable cow horses and expected his horses to be well-broke, usable and safe. Bucking and wild riding were discouraged, and a cowboy caught bucking his horse could expect to be fired.

In 1941, Mitchell bought a Thoroughbred stallion named Reminiscence, as well as a Quarter Horse colt named Lucky Strike, by Little Joe, from the CS Ranch, which later would be home to Mitchell's daughter, Linda, when she married Les Davis, who ran the outfit. Mitchell used Lucky Strike on the Bell mares. The Quarter Horse Mitchell was happiest about, however, was a colt purchased from the King Ranch, which, at that time, was developing what would become known as the "Old Sorrel" line, an exceptional family of working Quarter Horses. All his life, Mitchell remained committed to breeding solid cow horses and Quarter Horses, and he was elected AQHA president in 1946.

With the exception of the stallions, every horse and mare was ranch-raised, and all wore the Bell brand on the left shoulder. Number brands on the horses' left hips corresponded to their sires. Just about every horse in the remuda was a sorrel with white stockings and streaks on his face, the color and markings for which the Bell had long been famous. Of 120 or so horses, only a few were bays, blacks or duns.

When a man went to work on the Bell Ranch in the early days, he was assigned a string of 10 to 12 horses for his own use, and he made sure always to remember the color, size, markings and names of his horses. Asking which ones were his was frowned upon. The horses became a cowboy's responsibility during the entire time the man worked on the ranch, and no one else rode those horses.

A cowboy might ask to trade one of his horses for another one, and the wagon boss might okay that, but trading horses among the cowboys was not permitted. Fairness was the main reason, since the experienced, older men would end up with all the solid horses, leaving the rank ones for younger, greener cowboys. Through the years, there has never been much turnover among Bell Ranch cowboys because of quality horses in the ranch remuda.

Cow-Savvy Athletes

Today, most Bell horses and mares show stout conformation coming from a horse purchased in 1989, Steel Harmon, a 1981 stallion by Scottish Harmon and out of Bold Angel. Although Steel Harmon is no longer on the Bell, his nine years on the ranch played a significant role in the present-day remuda. Bloodlines in the mare band include Capital Letters, Figure Four Fritz and Docs Hickory.

Carroll Jack Lewis grew up around the Bell Ranch. His father worked there from 1974 to 1979. Later, he spent the summers of 1988 and '89 as part of the Bell crew. After stints at the Texas Panhandle's Tule and JA ranches, Carroll Jack accepted the Bell Ranch wagon boss position in 2000. Since then, he has focused on, among other things, raising versatile, strong ranch horses that weigh between 1,150 and 1,200 pounds.

"In the past, horses were just tools to be used on the ranch and were limited on ability and cow sense. Each horse had its specialty, whether it be roping, cutting or being able to travel on a long circle, but very few could do it all. Nowadays, on big ranches, the guys not only need to be good cowboys, but also good horsemen because we want something to sell in the end. We need to have the public in mind at the end of the trail," the wagon boss stressed.

Three years ago, he discovered a stallion that exhibited "athletic cow sense that can also go a long way." Justa Swinging Hick, a

Carroll Jack Lewis separates ranch mares from their foals.

107

7-year-old stallion by Docs Hickory and out of Justa Swinging Peanut, was acquired in a trade for a few ranch geldings. Justa Swinging Peanut also produced the 2001 National Cutting Horse Association Horse of the Year, Justa Smart Peanut. Unfortunately, Justa Swinging Hick died of colic in August 2006, but not before he sired two solid crops of ranch horses.

The ranch currently boasts a total of 200 horses, including a remuda of 100 mounts and 23 broodmares. The ranch also stands three stallions: Smokes Pago Pago, by Smoke Fifty with Tom The Barber on the bottom side; 3-year-old Ladys Bay Gun, by Dualin Gun and out of Playboys Lady Too, a granddaughter of Freckles Playboy; and the recently acquired Little Wars Blaze, by Little War O Lena and out of Doxie Bars Blaze.

"There is a nice ranchy look to him," Carroll Jack said of Little Wars Blaze, "and he will fit well with our horse program."

The Bell Broodmares

According to Carroll Jack, attitude is the No. 1 consideration in keeping broodmares, followed by conformation. Before going into the mare band, every filly is ridden for 30 days to assess her ability. The ranch keeps the best and sells the rest as started fillies.

"You don't know about their abilities and attitudes until you start riding them," the wagon boss declared.

All mares are pasture-bred with an 80 to 90 percent success rate, producing a crop of about 20 foals each year. Each mare band consists of 10 to 12 head, and one stallion is kept with each band. The foals run free in this land of vast pastures and rugged canyons, where they develop stamina, good feet, muscle and bone, all necessary qualities when a hard day's work is on the agenda. Mountain lions, however, remain a problem and claim the lives of up to four foals each year.

"We always look for signs," said the wagon boss of the predatory cats.

Typically, foals are branded in August. Each is given a brand designating its sire, and all foals also are marked with a year brand, so that any horse's age easily can be determined.

Weaning time is typically about mid-October. Weaning takes place at the mule pens, a set of corrals located in what is known as the Mule Pasture. At weaning,

Despite taking innovative approaches to raising cattle through the years, the Bell Ranch still believes in traditional cowboy ways.

the sun starts warming the grasslands just as Carroll Jack and his crew lope toward a red mesa to gather the mares and their foals. The sound of the horses' hooves quickly fades away as they soon disappear among the thickets. The cowboys' knowledge of the horses' habits and the lay of the land help the crew to easily locate the herd, and the cowboys' distant whistles and yelps become muffled by the thick brush.

Then comes a distant whinny. Soon, the entire mare band, foals glued to their mothers' sides, gallops from the brush toward the pens, the cowboys in tow. The low rumbling of running horses grows louder as they approach. A few minutes later, the herd is penned inside the corral, and the wagon boss takes a quick count.

Then Carroll Jack and his crew start the weaning process, cutting out small bunches at a time and urging the horses through an alleyway. There, a cowboy activates a system of gates to separate each mare from her foal and direct each into separate pens. The pace is fast, but the animals' safety remains the cowboys' No. 1 priority. Should a mare and her foal refuse to be separated, one cowboy ropes the dam while his teammate urges the youngster to an adjoining pen.

Once the separation process is finished, the mares are turned loose while the foals are trailered back to the ranch headquarters. There, they are turned out in a pen for a few days and fed alfalfa and grain. The ranch crew believes in abruptly weaning foals, considering that method less stressful than others.

"The faster we get the colts away from the mares, the easier it is on them," Carroll Jack said.

Ranch Remuda School

Later, the recently weaned youngsters are turned into a bigger area for several months. The following spring, it is time to separate the colts from the fillies to avoid inbreeding.

"It is sometimes harder to separate them after they've been running together for several months," Carroll Jack explained about the young horses. "It's like doing two weanings."

Typically, the colts are halter-broke as yearlings, with horseback cowboys roping the young horses and slipping a halter on each youngster.

Whenever cattle are gathered, any ranch-raised youngster is expected to carry his weight until the work is done.

The weanlings are hauled to the ranch headquarters and turned out for a few days in a corral before being turned into a larger lot for a few weeks.

"It's easier on the horses, and they learn to lead more quickly by doing it this way," Carroll Jack said.

Then each colt is taken to an adjoining pen, where another cowboy afoot takes over to work with the young horse. When the colts are 2 years of age, during a span of a couple of weeks, they are started under saddle. Then they are turned out for another couple of weeks until their training starts again. Every effort is made to handle the young horses as quietly as possible and to keep them from bucking. Nowadays, typically, each cowboy is given two colts as part of his string of six to eight horses, and he is responsible for their training.

Throughout the remainder of the summer, the young horses are used to ride small circles on cattle, as they get used to slickers and ropes, tools of the cowboy trade. The young horses are kept in the remuda, where they become accustomed to the rope corral and the routine of being roped out of it. By the time a young horse is 4, he needs to earn his keep and work a full day.

The ranch training method is based on the concept of "making the wrong things less easy for the horse," according to Lewis. He believes in riding every horse as an individual because the same method does not always fit every horse. What he reads in a horse determines whether he will ride the horse that day or not. Groundwork is part of each horse's training process, but so is cowboy logic.

'If you're not planning on riding the horse that day, why put a saddle on his back?" Carroll Jack commented.

Fond Memories

The ranch's horse program and training methods have yielded results. Bell Ranch cowboys have developed a quality remuda of tough horses that can get jobs done, as well as several very outstanding cow horses. Some such outstanding mounts have not only been paramount in establishing the Bell's reputation as a fine cow-horse producer, but also have left their marks on the cowboys who rode them.

George Ellis remembered a couple such horses he had ridden. "Chigger certainly tops my list as the smartest and most lovable horse I have ever ridden. Out of a Bell mare by an

Underwood stud, he was a little sorrel and never weighed more than 950 pounds. He could do everything but talk English. He was not the best cutting horse, but I never asked him to do anything he couldn't and didn't do cheerfully. I took him direct from the bronc breaker, and no one ever rode him except me until Jan, our daughter-in-law, fell in love with him; then I let her ride him. In his later years, the grandchildren also rode him. He was the only horse I ever rode that I was not the least bit afraid of. He would buck a few jumps sometimes, but I knew I could ride him, and he knew it too."

"A little bay called Runt was the best cutting horse I ever rode," George continued. "Ralph gave him to our son, George Jr., when George was only 12 years old. Runt was gentle. During most of the year, when George was away in school, I rode Runt. He was the proudest little horse and took great pride in his work. When you are working in the roundup and you start to cut a certain cow, many horses have trouble figuring out which cow you want, and many lose her if she rims around a little—but not Runt. Once you started one, he never lost her.

"One day, he and I started out with a silly, old dry cow, and she did a good deal of dodging around. At the edge of the roundup, she saw a little group of cattle standing just a little off from the main bunch. She made a dash for them, thinking to run through them and get back in the herd. I thought it would be fun to leave Runt alone and see what he would do, so I never moved the reins. He just darted around to the right place and was waiting for that cow when she tried to break back into the roundup," George said.

"When Runt dodged with a cow, you had better screw down in the saddle, for he would stop or turn just before you expected him to. This is the sign of a good cow horse—one that stops or turns a split second before you think he will."

Sculptor Curtis Fort cowboyed on the Bell during the 1960s. He still remembers the names of all the horses in his string, but some of his fondest memories go to a horse named Porticito.

"One of my favorites was Porticito, who was my top horse for doing work when it really counted. I never used him on big circles, but always caught him when we had heavy stock to rope. He was big and stout, but could sure move out. Whoever broke him put a good handle on him. He had a lot of heart and never quit me. Like a lot of ranch horses, he wasn't flashy-looking, and he'd never been to town and ridden in a parade so people could see him. He just did honest work every day that he was saddled. In my opinion, he deserves the world's

The Bell Ranch name and brand come from the bell-shaped mountain that marks the ranch's center.

admiration far more than any mount those Rose Bowl Parade punchers ride."

Other horses, although good, tough cow ponies, sometimes left painful memories with the cowboys who rode them, including George Ellis. "I had a horse called, oddly enough, Mary Lou. When Ralph gave him to me, I was told he might buck; and if he did, he would be hard to ride. I rode him for 10 years and always gave him all the hard rides because he could take them. However, I finally got to feeling sorry for him and started using him for a cow horse. He was a good one.

"In June 1954 we had a roundup to gather at Seco Corrals, and I caught Mary Lou to work the herd," George continued. "I had been cutting on him for perhaps 30 minutes and thought I had him warmed up real well when, suddenly, he blew up. I never had a horse buck so hard; he threw me sky-high. I landed on my back, and it knocked the wind out of me. The fall also broke three ribs."

George added, "The next morning, my ribs were hurting like fury, but I went to the wagon. It was moving time, so I told Buster to take the wagon on to Cow Pass Corrals. I would stay behind, as I thought we might have 'dogied' some calves the day before. I caught my horse, Batter, because he was the easiest trotting horse I ever rode. I paired up a couple of cows and calves, and then started slowly toward the wagon at Cow Pass. Every step hurt, but we made it. It was about eight miles."

Bell Traditions

Although the Bell always has been known for its innovative approach to ranching, the old-time cowhand traditions are still alive on this outfit, where most of the work still is done horseback. As manager Rusty Tinnin used to say, "This land is hard on horses and women."

Although horses now are trailered more from pasture to pasture than in the old days, a good horse is still the preferred mode of transportation. From the time the remuda is brought in by two wranglers in the early morning, tradition prevails. Once in the corral, the horses face outward, as they have been trained. Wagon boss Carroll Jack Lewis ropes each cowboy's mount for the day with a houlihan throw and leads the horse to the cowboy, who slips on a bridle.

In true Southwestern fashion, the Bell cowboys seem to favor full, thick leggings to fend off the dense brush and the always-prevalent rattlers. In addition, rawhide tapaderos cover stirrups to protect the cowboys' feet from hard mesquite and cholla cactus thorns. The

Horseshoes rest on a rail in the old barn on the Bell.

rest of the cowboys' attire is typical of the Southwest cowpunchers—wide-brimmed hats with the brim pulled high on the sides, high-topped boots and long-shanked spurs with big-spoked rowels.

One noticeable difference about cowboying in the Southwest—the pace. Cowboys need to work faster here than in other places because of the heat.

"We need to get all the work done in the morning, so when we ride somewhere, we need to get there fast. We've got to beat the heat," Carroll Jack stressed.

As with most big outfits, branding is the favorite time of the year on the Bell. In June, for three weeks to a month, a crew of about 12 cowboys goes out with the wagon and the remuda. They gather, brand, vaccinate and castrate the calves. Camp is established for three or four days, until every calf in the area has been branded. Then, Carroll Jack and his crew break camp and pull the wagon again.

In the past, the chuck wagon has been pulled by four big dun horses, well-matched in color and size, who could pull the wagon at a trot all the way to the next camp if the road permitted. But eventually, the old horse-drawn wagon wore out, and so did the horses that pulled it. It also became harder to find a cook who could drive four horses. Today, the wagon is an old four-wheel-drive army truck equipped with a water tank and a butane stove and refrigerator. The old horse-drawn wagon was donated to the Museum of New Mexico in Santa Fe, where it remains.

During branding, by 5 a.m. each morning two wranglers have trotted out to gather the remuda. Although still dark, the jingling sound of one or two "bell" horses has helped wranglers locate the herd.

Once the remuda has been penned in the rope corral, Carroll Jack and another hand catch the mounts for the day. Each cowboy walks to the corral and calls the name of the horse he wants for that day. A roper then catches the horse and calls his name. The rider steps over the rope into the corral, bridles his horse and leads him from the corral for saddling.

The sun is just peeking above a ridge when the cowboys, with Carroll Jack in the lead, take off at a hard trot for the day's work. Branding is done the old-fashioned way, by heeling and dragging the calves to the fire. Two ropers at a time work in the branding pen while three or four sets of flankers wrestle an average of 150

Thick, full chaps and rawhide tapaderos protect a rider's legs and feet from the thorny New Mexico brush.

to 200 calves a day. The remaining riding horses are hobbled outside the branding pen.

The man using the knife straps a nail bag with two pockets around his waist. One pocket is used for the bags cut from the bull calves, and the other is used for the ends of the heifer calves' ears. At day's end, the bags and ears are counted to determine how many calves were branded.

Bell Ranch Personalities

Through the years, the Bell Ranch's rugged beauty has attracted and inspired many notable artists and writers. In the 1940s, famed photographer Harvey Caplin shot many black-and-white photos portraying the Bell cowboys at work. Some of these photos have been used as the quintessential western iconography to promote the Stetson Hat Company.

Cholla are scattered across the Bell Ranch.

Later, the 1950s television show *Rawhide* utilized the Bell Ranch panoramas in its scenes. More recently, ad campaigns shot on the ranch have even included some of the Bell cowboys. Plus, New Mexico cowboy artist Gary Morton found inspiration for his paintings portraying cowboy life while working at the Bell during the 1970s.

Employee longevity seems to be among the Bell Ranch's trademarks, as traditions were established and perpetuated by men who served the spread for many years. Mike Slattery, the Bell's first general manager, was 16 years old when he left his hometown of New York City and ventured west in 1859. He started working at the Bell in 1869 and faithfully rode for the brand for 25 years. With a reputation for being as reckless and brave as he was a diligent worker, the hard-riding Slattery must have been equal to the conflicts he confronted during his regime, well able to endure through dangerous and unsettled times.

Mark Wood first drew Bell wages in 1919, and by the time the ranch was divided in 1947, he had served as wagon boss for 23 years. Ralph Bonds, who worked for the Bell a total of 48 years, was in charge of Mark's remuda. Moises Romero, however, had the longest tenure of all. He went to work for the Bell as a boy on the haying crew in the 1880s. By the 1890s he was drawing pay as a cowboy, and he continued riding for the Bell even after acquiring his own spread nearby. Moises died after the fall work of 1946, becoming a legend in the Bell's history.

The cowboys often appreciated a wagon boss during the 1960s, Leo Turner, who always asked them to do things in the nicest, most polite, old-fashioned ways. Rather than giving a direct order, he would say: "Joe, if you and Curtis don't mind, why don't y'all trot over to the Sabinoso and prowl through the

Some buildings at the ranch headquarters date back to the 1890s.

heifers. And, if you have time on your way back, come through the West Bronc pasture and see if that windmill is keeping up on water."

However, many itinerant cowboys were hired at branding and roundup time, and seldom was an inquiry made into a man's past history. Texas-born Black Jack Ketchum and his brother Sam, who came along at the end of the Waddingham-Slattery era, were examples of such one-time employees. Black Jack was a good cowhand, but occupied his time between cowboy jobs by holding up trains and in the process killed between 20 and 30 men. Eventually caught during an unsuccessful train robbery, he was sentenced to hang.

Through the years many good hands and colorful characters have left their marks on the Bell. Some might even have left a little bit of their souls behind. For those, the Bell was home.

Nonetheless, while the crew adheres to traditional cowboy philosophies and methods, the Bell Ranch continues to make improvements. Just as the ranch has been innovative in developing cattle programs, the Bell certainly has not allowed its horse program to fall behind the times. Thanks to such outfits, the range-riding cowboy lives on and each one passing through the Bell proudly becomes part of the myth.

Bell Ranch Timeline

1824: Former Spanish army captain Pablo Montoya was granted about 700,000 acres in the New Mexico territory.

1867: Montoya's attorney, John S. Watts, gained title to the land, but sold it three years later to Canadian land speculator Wilson Waddingham.

1875: Waddingham registered the "Bell" brand.

1886: Bell Ranch manager Mike Slattery put 140 miles of barbed-wire fencing around the Bell range.

1894: New York financiers John Greenbough and James Brown Potter took over the Bell Ranch.

1899: The Red River Valley Company, based in New Haven, Conn., provided stability on the Bell for almost the next 50 years.

1901: The Bell Ranch established a purebred Shorthorn herd.

1914: The ranch established a registered Hereford herd.

1932: Charles O'Donel, ranch manager since 1898, retired. He had installed the ranch's first windmills and telephone lines, and embraced an innovative concept—marketing Bell cattle as yearlings.

1933: Albert K. Mitchell, later an American Quarter Horse Association president, became ranch manager and held the position until the outfit's 1947 sale. He improved the ranch horse program and opted to market Bell cattle as weaner calves, setting yet another industry standard.

1947: The ranch was divided and sold in six large parcels. Harriet E. Keeney bought the brand and the 130,855-acre headquarters unit, which became known as the Bell Ranch, and hired George Ellis to run the outfit.

1970: Manager George Ellis, who began 205-day beef-performance studies, retired from the Bell. The ranch headquarters building was placed on the National Register of Historic Places. William N. Lane purchased the Bell Ranch, as well as the northern Waggoner acreage, previously sold in 1947, to effectively double the Bell Ranch's size.

1986: Don Hofman, who had managed the Bell since 1970, retired. Rusty Tinnin, who helped develop the Red Bell cattle breed, became ranch manager.

1989: The ranch purchased Steel Harmon, a 1981 stallion by Scottish Harmon, which had a significant impact on the ranch remuda.

2000: Carroll Jack Lewis became wagon boss on the Bell Ranch.

2006: With Rusty Tinnin's death, Bert Ancell, who had worked on the Bell since age 16, stepped into the manager's position.

7

CS CATTLE COMPANY

By Tim O'Byrne

The single-story, white ranch house rests on a solid foundation under the cottonwood trees. More than a century of ranching history and precious family memorabilia carefully are stored inside the thick protective walls, safe from the harsh elements known to ravage this corner of New Mexico's high-desert cow country. In the square structure's center, a small, elegant outdoor courtyard is surrounded by the four connecting house sections, each added through the decades to signify growth in the lives of the pioneering family who started the outfit in 1873, and still owns it to this day.

The CS uses only ranch-raised fillies as broodmare replacements to maintain and balance cow sense and athletic ability with size, conformation and temperament.

117

Rancher Linda Davis has spent a lifetime dealing with whatever comes her way, from slumping cattle markets and emergency medical situations to hall-of-fame induction ceremonies.

In the cool shade, not 10 feet from the kitchen door, sits an old water pump on a concrete slab covering a rainwater cistern. Traditional mechanical pumps incorporate a jack handle. This one does not. Its decorative steel cover, layered with whitewash, shields a heavy flat chain adorned with tiny water cups the size of homemade biscuits. A crank handle, like that used to start a Model T, channels the chain and its empty cups down into the well, returning with fresh, sweet water.

That this unique pump sits at the heart of the CS Cattle Company property is fitting. Water is life, especially to those who dare establish themselves as cattle ranchers in this desperately dry land. But of deeper significance is how the machine performs its simple function and the parallels that can be drawn between the pump and the family that operates the ranch.

The flat chain brings to mind the family's strength, worn somewhat thin from steady use, but in no danger of breaking. The cups suggest the family members' unity in achieving common goals. One by one, from the cistern's dark depths, each cup delivers its precious cargo. Alone, one tiny cupful seems insignificant, hardly enough to water a daisy. But together, with a bit of time and perse-

verance, those same tiny cups can fill a rain barrel.

A Large Western Land Grant

The southeastern slopes of the massive Sangre de Cristo (Spanish for "blood of Christ") Mountains spread their dark green fingers toward the Great Plains' expanse. More than half the mountain range stretches north into Colorado, the other half as far south as Sante Fe, New Mexico. Native cultures prospered and disappeared in the shadow of these mountains—the mysterious Anasazi, Utes and Jicarilla Apaches. The mountain range has changed little through the millennia, but control of the land was systematically and often brutally challenged by Spain, Mexico and Texas. Eventually, as part of the 1848 Treaty of Guadalupe Hidalgo that culminated the 1846 Mexican-American War, the area was ceded to the United States and christened the New Mexico Territory.

But the CS Ranch story begins a few years before the historic treaty, back in 1841, when Mexico still had the southwestern United States in its possession. Guadalupe Miranda and Charles Beaubien, following customary procedures brought to the New World from

Spain, asked the Santa Fe governor for title to a land grant, a large one, near the present-day town of Cimarron, N.M. The untamed country's settlement and economic prosperity were virtually ensured when a land grant was successful. After acquiring the grant, the pair began their venture to raise crops and livestock.

At roughly the same time, trapper and hunter Lucien Maxwell hired on with John C. Fremont's 1842 expedition to chart the West. Kit Carson was an expedition guide, and Maxwell began a friendship with the legendary frontiersman that lasted throughout their lives. Maxwell's travels took him through the land-grant area, where he met and married Charles Beaubien's daughter, Luz, in 1844. Maxwell continued to accompany Fremont and Carson on subsequent expeditions, but in 1847 settled in Cimarron with his wife and her family, and began to assume his father-in-law's responsibilities in managing the grant.

During the next 25 years, the now-famous Maxwell land grant accumulated more than 1,750,000 acres, making it one of the largest such land grants in U.S. history. By all accounts Maxwell was a respected man in the community. He spent several years as postmaster and Indian agent in Cimarron before selling his massive land grant in 1870 for $1,350,000. A group of English investors intended to operate the holding under the name of Maxwell Land Grant and Railway Company, or MLG.

The grant later changed hands to another investment group from the Netherlands, and Frank Springer, senior partner and legal counsel of the new investment company, assumed the position of company president. A complex series of events, not uncommon to large-scale entrepreneurial efforts in the West, required Frank to spend a great deal of his time and energy during the next decade defending the new company's interests. When the enterprise faced imminent restructuring in the late 1870s, Frank settled his remuneration request by accepting title to 200,000 acres of the original Maxwell land grant.

Those 200,000 acres would become the CS Cattle Company.

The Sign on the Door

Years ago, a brass plaque etched with the words "Office of Charles Springer Cattle Co." was fastened to a ranch building door. "CS," the registered brand still in use after

Company president since his father's death in 2000, J. Kirk Davis shares a goal with his siblings—keeping the CS outfit together.

Randy Davis runs the hunting camps on the CS and cowboys whenever necessary, as well.

Georgia native Mary Davis, whose husband, Warren, is CS cowboss, now manages the ranch's horse program.

13 decades, is derived from Springer's initials. Today, the office door is weathered, its plaque beautifully aged like a ship's bell, and many noteworthy cattlemen and -women have passed through this humble threshold since 1873.

The Springer family operated the ranch hands-on throughout the remainder of the 19th century and well into the 20th, with horses emerging as a major trading interest. In 1885, Frank Springer initiated a serious breeding program. He purchased the French Thoroughbred stallion Uhlan, along with two English-bred stallions and 12 fillies, at a sheriff's dispersal sale of the MLG stallion line, an ill-fated venture begun by William Sherwin, the flamboyant and short-termed MLG president.

Hank Springer, Frank's son, set the tone for the next century with his 1912 purchase of an outstanding sorrel stallion known as "Little Joe." The very foundation of the American Quarter Horse Association was built on the progeny of this horse and others like him.

The CS Ranch, as did many Western outfits with enough range to run large horse herds and the skilled horsemen to saddle them, entered into long-term arrangements

Davis family members and the CS crew are known for their finesse in handling both horses and cattle.

to supply the U.S. Army Western Remount Services with horses. The contracts ran from the 1920s until the beginning of World War II, with the government supplying top-notch Thoroughbred stallions to breed to the high-quality CS mares.

During the 1930s, Ed Springer, regarded by many as the "Father of Racing in New Mexico," started the ranch's successful Thoroughbred racehorse-breeding program. During the next few decades, the CS won many prestigious races, including derbies and futurities for New Mexico-bred horses. In addition to the remounts, racing horses, and foundation Quarter Horses used for cow work, the Springers also bred and trained amazing, agile polo ponies and even hunter-jumper horses for discriminating event riders.

By 1930, the ranch broodmare band totaled more than 200 head, and the horse production program remained at the forefront of the ranch's economic-management plan until the end of World War II, which changed the face of North American commerce forever. Beef cattle eventually took over that top economic spot. In the years to come, the Springer name would give way, as well, to that of another family branch, whose members would devote their lives to the beloved ranch their predecessors had built from scratch.

Les Davis Takes The Reins

During the CS Cattle Company's formative years, Springer family relatives had become established in Philadelphia, Penn. Frank Springer's daughter, Ada, had married Warren B. Davis, a prominent reconstructive surgeon and surgery professor at Jefferson Medical School. Their second son, James Leslie, or "Les," was set to follow in his father's footsteps and already had completed premed studies at Dartmouth College. But the young man's adventurous spirit soon emerged.

In a 1941 letter to his bachelor uncle, Ed Springer, who had managed the New Mexico ranch for many years, Les inquired about the possibility of coming to visit and perhaps staying awhile. Ed wrote back, telling his nephew to come, and "awhile" turned out to be the rest of Les' life, interrupted only by his World War II service commitment.

Shortly after the United States entered the war in December 1941, Les left the CS Ranch's relative sanctuary, signing up for active duty in the Army. He wanted action,

and he saw it. His European tour as a tank forward observer earned him three Purple Hearts, the Bronze Star and a Presidential Unit Citation. Two tanks were blown violently from beneath him, but his company's mission, "to take Bastogne at all costs," became more than enough reason to live. Long after the last shot was fired in 1945, pieces of shrapnel continued to menace Les' body, and did so until his last days.

After his 1947 Army release, Les decided to return to manage the ranching operation for his aging uncle, Ed. Les assumed the roles of CS Ranch president and board chairman when the elderly gentleman passed away in 1964. That Les had found his calling is an understatement. The only thing missing was a family with whom to share the ranch. Soon that, too, would change.

When a cowboy rides for an outfit such as the CS, his gear often honors a longtime association.

When Linda Showed Up

"C'mon, Suzy," Linda Davis called in a motherly tone.

She was talking to a cow as her gentle-natured sorrel horse kept the pace, allowing Linda to concentrate on moving the cattle she enjoys so much. The cows respectfully fell in line.

"Come on," she said again, but to no particular cow.

The cows have heard that same reassuring refrain a million times before. So has the family. It is Linda's trademark. Every good cowhand has one, and Linda obviously is very good. Raised by her father, former Bell Ranch manager Albert K. Mitchell, this intelligent, caring woman learned at an early age how to ranch, and how to do it right.

"Dad taught us how to do everything gentle," recalled Linda, reflecting on her relationship with the remarkable man considered a legend in the West. "But he also taught us how to look a person in the eye when we shake his hand."

A former president of the American Hereford Cattle Breeders Association, a founding member of the American Quarter Horse Association, and a New Mexico state representative, Mitchell was considered a visionary thinker in the cattle and horse industries.

When Linda was 4 years old, her mother died, and nurturing her siblings became a prerequisite to family survival. That instinct has served Linda well through the years.

In 1953, Linda married Les, who was known to remark, "Things got a whole lot better on the CS the day Linda showed up."

He realized she was not the sort of woman who would just get by on the high-desert cattle ranch he had come to love; he knew she would contribute her very best. This attribute, this willingness to contribute, sets great people apart from others, and the West is full of such people. A ranching and farming community is not something to enjoy only when the mood strikes; the strength and commitment of neighbors working together sometimes can be a matter of life and death. Although Linda and Les worked hard to keep the ranch afloat while raising a family of six devoted children, there was still something left to give back to the community.

Snowcapped mountains provide scenic backdrops for much of the CS Cattle Company work.

"We had the only station wagon in the country," Linda recalled, thinking back to a day when transportation flow, compared to that of today, was minimal. "Anytime there was a medical emergency and they needed to transport somebody to the hospital, we'd get the phone call because there were no ambulances anywhere around."

Using an old kitchen door as a backboard and rolls of bandages to tie things together, Linda and Les hauled many a poor, broken-legged cowpuncher to town in their old station wagon. Today, Linda is a trained emergency medical responder and has been instrumental in setting up a training program for similar area responders.

Chinks are well-suited for the often hot and dry New Mexico climate.

When the modern highway system developed in this region of the country, high-speed accident rates went up accordingly, as did the seriousness of injuries. Trained emergency responders, who can efficiently tend to an accident scene, greatly increase any victim's chance of survival here in this remote portion of New Mexico.

Davis Family Ties

Large families are not uncommon in ranching circles, and ranches always have been fantastic places to raise children. Where else can a child eat, sleep, work and play side-by-side with parents and grandparents, or experience enough job diversity to choose one that suits him, whether it involves mechanics, cattle, horses or cooking?

Eldest son Warren Davis is the cowboss. "Dad never pushed us to take over the ranch, or return to it," Warren said, while prowling through placid black cattle on late fall grass. His horse was intent, but stood comfortably. "There was never any of that pressure. He told us to go to college so we'd have something to fall back on."

J. Kirk Davis is company president. A self-confessed mechanically inclined person, he still would be welcomed on any cowboy crew in the country. When he's not horseback doing ranch work or tending to some mechanical issue, J. Kirk can be found in the office at the CS Ranch headquarters, just off Highway 58 east of Cimarron.

"Keeping the outfit together is not easy," J. Kirk admitted. But working through the challenges that always threaten to break up family ranches, such as the CS, is a goal the Davis children passionately share.

After Les passed away in 2001, the family scattered his ashes on a ridge just south of the headquarters site. "Part of his soul is up on that ridge," J. Kirk commented, "and I couldn't imagine another owner not driving by that place with reverence."

The potentially devastating estate tax levied on family members inheriting a working farm or ranch leads a long list of concerns that J. Kirk and his sister, Julia Davis Stafford, monitor on behalf of the Davis family and the CS. Estate planning, environmental issues and the ranch's co-existence with water and natural habitat concerns can require a great deal of time and energy, especially for a family defending entirely deeded land defined as such more than a century ago.

This ranch horse, taking a break between jobs, must be willing to work cattle and maintain a calm head when there is work to be done.

During dry years, the ranch sometimes must reduce its mother-cow herd numbers.

Although ranch diversification might seem a new concept, one look at the CS Cattle Company's historic past proves that untrue. Years before, the Springers had diversified their operation by participating in the U.S. Army Remount breeding program. Today, diversity is a fact of Western life; every little bit helps, as the Davis family has learned through the years.

With complete control of their 150,000 acres of pristine raw prairie, foothills and mountainous grazing land, the family shares its treasure with a select group of qualified hunters. They not only appreciate the opportunity to hunt for trophy elk and deer, but also treat the land with the respect it deserves.

Randy Davis, the second son, assumed the role of manager of the hunting operation in 1982. When he isn't on a hunt, he cowboys whenever and wherever the family needs him.

Bruce Davis, who also serves as marketing manager for cattle sales, manages the mountain country stretching from the Great Plains and into the Sangre de Cristos' eastern slopes.

Daughter Kim Davis Barman has developed the ranch's herd health program. She also has introduced key holistic resource-management concepts to the outfit and pioneered the development of planned grazing and sustainable ranching practices on the CS.

The CS Ranch Horses

Warren's wife, Mary, a Georgia native and accomplished horsewoman, is responsible for the outfit's horse program. Mary's breeding and training philosophies are simple, yet effective: The CS horses need to go to work. She likes their remuda to be calm thinkers, capable of any task, but willing to work with level heads. The CS conformation type was set years ago through longtime cow foreman Jiggs Porter's careful breeding practices, and the ranch has tried to keep those bloodlines current without compromising the foundation.

Currently CS mares are bred to Roosters Shorty, by Gallo del Cielo and out of Shorty Lena Six, and to Mr Remind, by Letters Reminder and out of Snoopers Sassy. Most recently, Desire Again, a grey son of the 2004 AQHA Superhorse Real Gun and out of

The New Mexico ranch's wide open spaces seem to dwarf horse, rider and herd.

Four connecting ranch house sections surround an inner courtyard at the headquarters.

Zans Diamond Desire, a two-time world champion in tie-down roping, has joined the stallion roster.

The mares balance breeding for cow sense and athletic ability through the lines of Continental King and Doc O'Lena, with size, conformation and temperament through the lines of General Delivery, Mr Blue Bar and, most recently, Desired Vision, a Blondy's Dude- and Sonny Dee Bar-bred stallion. The CS uses only ranch-raised fillies as replacements in the broodmare band, which typically produces about 10 foals annually.

The CS Ranch usually maintains about 40 head in the working remuda. These capable ranch horses can be equally adept in the competitive arena. They occasionally have proven their worth whenever a Davis family member wants to back into a roping box. Mary also competes on a limited basis in Ranch Horse Association of America-sanctioned events.

The CS Cattle Operation

That same quiet-handling philosophy applies to the CS cow herd, just as it does to the CS horses. Late one morning a few hundred head of dry cows along a distant fence line needed to be gathered. Linda had no intention of watching the work from a pickup's comfort. She and her family put on a display of horse- and cattle-handling finesse that could serve as premium instructional material for anyone who works with livestock and wants to enjoy a great day.

The CS cows are well trained through repetitive positive reinforcement, the same tactics used in successful child-rearing and colt-starting. The cattle respect the cowboys and cowgirls and, as with the horses, are unafraid of working scenarios.

Due to years of ongoing drought, CS cow numbers have been reduced in recent years to about 1,400 head, which includes 200 or so replacement heifers. Calves are sold primarily on video although the occasional odd lot might go through the sale barn at nearby Clayton, N.M., or in Dalhart, Texas. However, some or even most of the calves might be held over as stocker cattle on the CS, where approximately 2,500 yearling steers can be brought in for a five- to six-month grazing season.

Tack Room Saddles and Ghosts

The CS Ranch tack room's white adobe walls are a foot thick. Bars cemented into the

The CS Cattle Company received the American Quarter Horse Association and Bayer Animal Health Best Remuda Award in 2000.

The old-time pump sits at the heart of the CS headquarters near Cimarron, N.M., where water is a treasured commodity.

129

windows create the feeling of an Old West jailhouse, yet it is cool and quiet inside. One almost can feel the ghosts of cowboys long gone, lingering among the saddles resting on racks along the wall and trading yarns about the old days. But the ghosts vanish into the rafters above when intruders from the bright outside world burst through the squeaky wooden door.

Les Davis, Ed Springer, Will James, Jiggs Porter—all veterans of the gramma grass plains, the wooded creek bottoms, the cactus-filled draws and the juniper ridges of the Sangre de Cristos. They are the ones who frequent this room. They were here, not so long ago. You'd swear. So many good horses are gone, too, their names and little quirks brought back to life only when the ghostly cowboys materialize to visit when nobody else is around.

Will James, artist and author of *Smokey the Cowhorse* and many Western novels, left his French-Canadian home as a young teen-ager, a rebellious, talented youth who needed little more than a break in life. James drifted through the West, punching cows wherever he could, learning the trade and soaking up the culture. His drawings ultimately became legendary in the close circle of Western ranchers.

When the young lad showed up at the CS in the early 1920s, Ed Springer took him in and gave him a job. Before long James' artistic abilities came to light, and Springer, with a little help from some associates, sent the lad to develop his gifts at a college in the East.

That worked for a while, but the halls of learning could not keep the young man's spirit in check. He broke free from academia after only a few months, but did not let down his sponsors. James had met his lifelong publisher during that short adventure back East, and the two were loyal to one another throughout the cowboy artist and author's entire career.

Nor did James ever forget Springer. Every year the talented kid, now a Western legend in his own right, sent a personally inscribed book to the grand old man as his way of saying, "Thanks."

Jiggs' Legacy

On the floor of a storage room connected to the tack shed sits a plain wooden box, its contents askew, as if it had been pulled out just that morning by a cowhand who needed some tool kept within. The inscription on the box reads "Jiggs Porter, CS Ranch, New Mexico."

Longtime cow foreman Jiggs Porter strongly influenced ranch horse conformation on the CS, as well as the bloodlines selected through the years.

"Jiggs always cut the colts the old way," J. Kirk explained, referring to the traditional technique of using a razor-sharp knife, a set of emasculators and a liberal dousing of iodine, "and this was always his cuttin' box. It'll always be his cuttin' box."

Today, Randy Davis performs this important task just as Jiggs taught him. And Randy draws his tools from that very same box, kept exactly where Jiggs last left it.

Jiggs showed up at the outfit in 1933 and stayed for longer than most men live. He remained on active duty until just a few months before his death in 2005. Although he eventually had to trade a horse for a pickup, he continued to ride for the brand. Following decades of continuous service, Jiggs was like the biggest shade tree in the yard—steadfast, deeply rooted, and able to withstand the storms that come and go with time. In their own quiet ways, the Davis family members truly honor and miss their mentor.

"He gave his soul and his life to the CS," J. Kirk said with deep respect and admiration. "When you worked for Jiggs, he expected a lot from you, and as a result, I suppose, I learned to expect a lot of others. He ran the show, there's no doubt about it, and he

wanted us kids to know every bit about punching cows that he knew."

Where The Future Takes Them

The CS Ranch still stands strong more than 130 years after Frank and Charles Springer's first calf crop was branded in 1874. That accomplishment might seem trite, almost a given, on the pages of a book or in a sterile museum showcase. What could possibly go

Jiggs Porter, who came to the CS in 1933 and remained until his death in 2005, left a lasting legacy.

In the early 1920s, Western artist and author Will James frequented this CS tack room, which remains in use today.

131

Five of Linda and Les Davis' children are involved with the ranch: (from left) Warren Davis, Julia Stoddart and Bruce, Randy and J. Kirk Davis. Sibling Kim lives in Albuquerque, N.M.

wrong to derail an apparently self-sustaining property handed down virtually unchallenged from generation to generation?

A lot. The CS story is not one of privilege, although time and circumstance have played roles in creating advantageous opportunities. Instead, the CS story resonates of hard work and sacrifice.

In the 1920s, when Springer descendants were faced with deciding about the future of a ranch that had grown dear to the family, they chose to keep it. That meant suffering a significant financial setback as they tidied up the loose ends of various business affairs. They simply could not dismiss their predecessors' visions and the years of toil they had endured to that point. And so it was with Les Davis.

"Dad never tried to force the ranch on any of us," J. Kirk reflected. "He always said that if it worked out, that we were someday interested in the outfit and it could be part of our lives in some way, then that would be just fine. If not, that would be okay, too."

Les' gift, then, was the opportunity for guilt-free assessment by each of the Davis siblings, to make their individual decisions and trust their instincts.

Now it's time for J. Kirk's generation to lay the same framework, but times have changed. Today's complex, ranch-inheritance tax structure challenges families faced with handing

CS horses take their ease in the soft New Mexico light, which, at times, can be harsh, hot and glaring.

The "CS" in the ranch name represents Charles Springer. His brother, Frank, was Les Davis' grandfather.

CS Ranch Timeline

1841: Mexican citizens Charles Beaubien and Guadalupe Miranda petitioned the Santa Fe governor to allow them title to a land grant in the Cimarron area.

1864: Charles Beaubien died, leaving much of his estate to son-in-law Lucien Maxwell, who purchased more property until what became known as the Maxwell Land Grant exceeded 1,700,000 acres.

1870: A company of English investors, the Maxwell Land Grant and Railway Company, known as MLG, paid Maxwell $1,350,000 for the properties.

1873: MLG hired attorney Frank Springer of Cimarron, N.M., to defend the land title. His remuneration package included 200,000 acres of the original grant. Frank and brother Charles established the Charles Springer Cattle Company, later known as the CS Cattle Company, whose brand is still in use today.

1873 – 1947: The Springer family, including Frank's sons, Hank and Ed, operated the ranch, raising horses and cattle.

1933: Jiggs Porter, longtime cow foreman, began an amazing career with the CS, which did not end until his death in 2005.

1947: James Leslie "Les" Davis, Frank Springer's grandson, took over as CS Ranch general manager.

1953: Les Davis married Linda Mitchell, daughter of distinguished cattleman and horseman Albert K. Mitchell, manager of the Bell Ranch and a founding member of the American Quarter Horse Association, as well as New Mexico state representative.

1950s – 1970s: Les and Linda Davis raised their six children, and the ranch prospered. In 1964, following Ed Springer's death, Les became CS Cattle Company president and chairman of the board, positions he held until his death in 2001.

2000: Les and Linda Davis were inducted into the Hall of Great Westerners at the National Cowboy and Western Heritage Museum in Oklahoma City, Okla. The CS Cattle Company received the American Quarter Horse Association and Bayer Animal Health Best Remuda Award.

2001: Les Davis, a decorated war hero and respected cattleman, passed away, and J. Kirk Davis, his son, assumed the role of corporate president.

property and management to the younger relatives willing to take lifelong risks. But no matter the Davis family's problems, its members remain focused on doing what they consider the right thing, which means avoiding the temptation of a massive sell-off for a quick return.

"Each generation of our family has made huge sacrifices to hold this outfit together," J. Kirk stated with conviction. "We have no intention of breaking it up. We're going to continue as a ranching operation, and the family is committed to staying together and making that happen."

University, Terry is intensely interested in pasture management.

"The native pastures do withstand drought better and provide grasses and forbs that mature at different times, which means they supply a more continuous source of feed, depending on moisture, for our cattle," Terry explained. "However, native grasses cannot tolerate as high a stocking rate as other forage, such as Bermuda grass, for example."

Terry's attention to pasture management is recognized throughout the state. In 2003, the Stuart Ranch received the Excellence in Range Management award from the Oklahoma Society of Range Management.

"We use fertilizer on the cultivated wheat and Bermuda grass pastures to increase the nutrient value of the plant. We also use burning and spraying to control mesquite, weeds and improve grazing conditions. You can never let up in this country on brush control, or you lose your grazing fast. In addition, the land near Caddo has more rainfall, which produces different types of brush that are even more difficult to clear."

It might seem unusual for a woman to run such a large ranching operation, but Terry comes by this ability naturally. Her family has deep ties to the land.

The Early Years

Established in 1868, the ranch today, with more than 40,000 acres of native grass and wheat pastures, is the oldest continuously operated family ranch in the state of Oklahoma. However, Stuart Ranch cattle no longer carry Robert Clay Freeny's CF brand, but a "7S" on the left hip, and horses carry "S" brands on their left shoulders. Terry's grandfather, Robert Terry Stuart, used the "Bar S" brand and, in fact, called the ranch the Bar S for a while. But Terry's father wanted a different brand, so a tail was added to the bar to form a 7. Today, all ranch horses have 7S in their names.

Robert Terry Stuart, Terry's paternal grandfather, was born in Texas, near Lawrence, in 1880. Soon, the young Stuart family moved to Decatur in Wise County, northwest of Fort Worth, where "R.T." grew up ranching. His parents wanted R.T. to go to college, and he did until a bout with malaria brought an end to his formal schooling. R.T. tried his hand at a number of occupations, but made his first real money hauling rock for $40 a month and 25 cents a yard. At the end of that job, he banked

Stuart Ranch horse-division manager Chris Littlefield has been with the outfit since 1999.

$10,000, seed money from which a mighty insurance company would be born.

The American insurance industry was just getting established at the time, and R.T. hired on with a fledgling company and soon found he had a knack for sales. At 28, he became president of his own company, American Home Life Insurance. Soon, R.T. sold the company and formed another, Bankers Trust Company, which he later sold when he bought Mid-Continent Life Insurance Company.

By the time he was in his early 30s, the rancher's son was a wealthy and influential man. But he never lost his love for the ranching way of life. In 1916, R.T. looked into Oklahoma land, liked what he saw and moved his company headquarters to Oklahoma City.

In Oklahoma in 1930, he met Ida Freeny, who had grown up in Freeny Valley, near Caddo in. R.T. and Ida married in 1931. His wife inherited her family homestead in the lush Oklahoma grasslands, where the Stuart

Sorting cattle is a way of life for Chris Littlefield, no matter if he's working cattle on the ranch or training a horse for competition.

Ranch began to unfold. The Stuarts' son, Robert Terry "Bob" Stuart Jr., not only would continue the ranching legacy his grandparents began, but also would build the insurance company his father had developed.

The Cattle Operation

"Dad never worked the ranch full-time because he had the insurance business to take care of," Terry explained. "But we spent as much time on the ranch as possible, and our family was here for most of the summer every year."

But through the years the cattle operation had suffered, and it was Bob Stuart's idea to hire his daughter to revitalize the program. At the time, Terry, who had been widowed when her now-grown sons were very young, had her own consulting business and developed management plans for other ranches. The call to manage the family ranch, however, was a dream come true.

"Being a rancher is all I've ever really wanted to be," she stated.

Today, she answers to a board of directors, who are part of the family corporation.

One of the first decisions Terry made was to shorten the calving season to 60 days in spring and fall. This compressed calving schedule has made it much easier to manage the herd and workload. In addition, the shorter season makes it more economical to feed cows, calves are more uniform in size, with smaller age differences between oldest and youngest, which helps marketing, and bulls can be utilized in two seasons. Despite caring for thousands of cattle, as well as horses to breed and train, the ranch gets by with about 10 full-time employees.

"More than 85 percent of the calves are born within the first 45 days of each season," Terry said. "That allows us to schedule our workload much more efficiently."

Fall calves are born in September and October, branded in December and weaned in May. These calves go to the feedlot at the end of June. Spring calves are born in March and April, branded in April and weaned in October. These calves go on wheat pastures prior to sale.

Stuart Ranch runs between 2,000 and 2,500 mother cows, depending on the weather and the pastured yearlings.

"In the winter we run our home-raised cattle on wheat, as well as the purchased yearlings," Terry explained. "In the summer the yearling situation is totally dependent on spring rains. We will run our heifers on grass, but most of the home-raised steers go to the feedlot at the end of June."

Drought conditions can result in herd reduction, if necessary, although Terry has worked hard to develop additional water sources. The ranch is totally dependent on surface water.

"I swore I'd never haul water to cattle," she said with a smile. "A friend told me once, 'The cattle work for you, you don't work for the cattle,' and I've never forgotten that."

To continue to improve the raised cattle's quality, Terry has concentrated on increasing the desirable traits through selective breeding. The ranch does purchase bulls, but they must meet stringent standards.

"We buy only bulls that conform to our expected progeny difference criteria, as well as fit our physical requirements for size and structure," Terry explained.

As on most large ranches, the hands are divided between the headquarters and camps scattered across the property. A new north camp, completed in 2006, handles spring

Chris Littlefield is adept at training and showing horses such as Seven S Heatwave, a Stuart-raised stallion now owned by J&J Cattle Company.

first-calf heifers and fall cows, and Terry continues to upgrade facilities at the other camps. A camp man takes care of a specific ranch area designated by management. This includes checking cattle, maintaining fences and pens, and doing anything else necessary in his area.

"Each camp man is responsible and accountable for his country," Terry added.

Today, the ranch is recognized for the quality beef cattle it produces. Cowboys and Terry are horseback to care for all the cattle, and the crew prides itself on the horses they make. Not ones to rest on past achievements, however, Terry and manager Chris Littlefield, a noted horseman and native Texan who joined the ranch in 1999, are committed to continually improving the horse herd, as well.

Raising Top Horses

Since its inception, the Stuart Ranch has bred outstanding Quarter Horses from the outfit's band of exceptional broodmares. Displaying the breed's versatility, Stuart horses have competed and won in show pens

year after year, as well as exhibiting the stamina and athletic ability so critical to ranch work. When Terry, an accomplished horsewoman and competitor herself, proved successful in managing the cattle program, her father asked her to assume responsibility for the horse operation, as well. She accepted the challenge.

Historically, the ranch always has had fine horses, with many of the original broodmares coming from Duard Wilson and the Waggoner Ranch in north-central Texas, across the Red River from Oklahoma. To enhance the mare lines, the ranch bought Big Shot Dun, by Pretty Boy, from the Waggoner Ranch in 1949. Pretty Boy's grandsire was the great foundation stallion Peter McCue, and this grandson was the beginning of the Stuart Ranch Quarter Horse breeding program.

The Stuarts continued to build their horse herd with the 1963 purchase of Son O Leo, by the legendary Leo and out of a Sugar Bars- and King-bred mare. Son O Leo was crossed repeatedly and successfully on Big Shot Dun daughters. The fillies from those breedings

Stuart Ranch horses— broodmares, as well as remuda geldings— reflect desirable traits the outfit's breeding program has targeted for years.

Ranch foals show the promise of things to come and the results of the outfit's well-considered breeding program.

crossed well with another outstanding ranch stallion purchased in 1980, the American Quarter Horse Association Champion Port Command, by Commander King.

The most prolific producer of Son O Leo breedings was the great mare Miss T Stuart, who raised a line of exceptional performers. Her offspring included AQHA Champions Seven S Sunset, Seven S Valentine and Seven S Taffy, a Superior western pleasure horse, as well as Seven S Suzanna, who earned Superiors in heading and heeling.

Miss T Stuart also produced Seven S Margarita, dam of AQHA junior heading world champion and Superhorse Genuine Redbud, as well as Genuine Hombre, who earned Superiors in reining, working cow horse, heading, heeling and tie-down roping. Seven S Genuine Miss, the first AQHA high-point ranch-versatility award-winner, with Superiors in heading and heeling, was a daughter of Seven S Margarita, and so was Genuine Jezabelle. She became an AQHA world show qualifier in heading and heeling, as did Seven S Genuine Zan, her foal by Seven S Zanaday, the 1992 world champion junior heading horse, who was used at stud with the Stuart broodmare band.

In 1995, the ranch received the Best Remuda Award from AQHA and Bayer Animal Health, further recognition of the excellent horses the Stuarts consistently produces.

A Change in Type

However, in recent years Terry and Chris have been changing the mare prototype for the Stuart horse program. Although early ranch mares represented a solid foundation Quarter Horse, through the years a different type horse has become popular.

"Our horses were established and recognized for their quality, but they represented old genetics and needed some modernization," Terry explained. "If we are truly breeders, and we believe we are, then each year's foal crop should be better than the last. Those older genetics have a place as a foundation for the future, but it was clear we needed to enhance our horses with modern blood. We needed horses that were a bit quicker and not

Shortened spring and fall calving seasons have made it easier to manage the cow herd, as well as the workload, on the Stuart Ranch.

quite so large, with big stops and plenty of intensity on a cow."

Terry credits Chris for helping her become more analytical about the horses the ranch kept, sold and purchased.

"People often get too emotionally attached to their horses to make the necessary changes and stay current," Chris commented. "It's easy for ranch programs to get behind the times. Terry was pretty sentimental about her horses, but she's also open-minded, which is what makes her so good at her job. She realized we needed to change the horse program in order to compete."

So the two managers developed a five-year plan for the Stuart horse program, based on the type of horse they wanted for ranch work, competition and breeding.

"Basically we wanted it all, and wrapped up in a pretty package, too," Terry declared.

In the past, the ranch produced outstanding rope horses, but Terry and Chris now wanted more versatile animals. This desire led them to breed horses they thought would do well in cutting and reined cow horse competition.

"We specifically bought mares that were producers and performers in cutting and reined cow horse," Terry explained. "But we were also very careful to buy only mares that fit our conformation standards, as well. We'll always be a ranch that strives for quality over quantity."

By increasing foal marketability with newer bloodlines, the ranch is able to sell more young horses.

"Any time you can sell colts and avoid training and keeping costs, that's good for business. We know exactly how much it costs to keep a horse and when we can make a profit," Terry stated emphatically.

Ranch Geldings

The ranch keeps some colts each year for its own use and runs about 24 geldings in the remuda. These horses are used for daily work with Terry and Chris riding those that might be destined for the show pen. Terry said the opportunity to use the competitive show horses on the ranch is mentally good for the horses. Plus, doing so helps her and Chris to evaluate the ranch-breeding program results on a daily basis.

The ranch is well-known for its quality ranch geldings. A contributing factor: As an

A hands-on manager, Terry Stuart Forst often is horseback working cattle, and always evaluates horse, cattle and pasture grasses as she works.

Alertly focused on the cattle, yet soft in hand, this bay demonstrates why Stuart Ranch horses are in demand.

incentive to make solid, responsive horses, a cowboy gets a percentage of the sale price whenever an older gelding is sold from his string.

The Bottom Side

Although the ranch hands ride geldings, Terry and Chris ride mares, as well. Every mare in the broodmare band is ridden before the decision is made to breed her. According to the managers, fillies are sold that do not meet their exacting criteria, but who will meet the needs of their new owners perfectly well.

Historically, the ranch has not kept any horse colts for breeding, as the bottom sides of their pedigrees are too closely related to those of the mares. Broodmares in the band represent such outstanding stallions as Shining Spark, Peppy San Badger, Grays Starlight and Dual Pep.

"We place a lot of emphasis on the bottom side of the pedigree," Terry explained. "We're looking for outcrosses that will breed back well to Real Gun. But the mares have to be good movers and demonstrate athletic ability, trainability, focus and intensity, and willingness on a cow before we consider them for breeding."

The ranch has 27 broodmares, as well as several recipient mares for embryo transfer. In addition to the desired performance characteristics Terry and Chris hope the mares pass along to their foals, the two top hands also evaluate ranch broodmares in other respects.

"We look at ease of breeding, as well as mothering and milking ability, as part of our mare evaluation, and a lot of breeders don't do that," Terry said.

Mares are bred on a natural cycle, and foals begin arriving in March. Mares are bred again starting around April 15th. The local veterinarian takes care of collecting and shipping semen, as well as artificially inseminating some mares.

The Real Deal

Chris, a superb horseman in his own right, has shown ranch stallions to Ranch Horse Association of America National Finals championships—Real Gun in 2002 and

Stuart Ranch runs between 2,000 and 2,500 mother cows, depending on the weather and number of pastured yearlings.

That's right—this Stuart Ranch cowboy is tied-on, his rope fast to his saddle horn, rather than dallied.

Seven S Genuine Zan in 2003. Real Gun, an eye-catching gray, earned the 2004 AQHA World Championship Show Superhorse title, a 2004 AQHA reserve world championship in senior working cow horse and the 2004 National Reined Cow Horse Association bridle-horse world title in the limited open division.

Real Gun, by Playgun, has quickly driven the Stuart Ranch horse-breeding program into the upper echelon of the Quarter Horse industry. All mares bred to Real Gun will have foals that are eligible as 4-year-olds for the NRCHA Stallion Stakes, and eligible for the AQHA Incentive Fund, the National Reining Horse Association Sire and Dam Program and the National Reining Horse Breeder's Classic.

"We're getting some really nice babies from Real Gun," Terry said. "We sold most of the first couple of foal crops as weanlings, but now are selecting the ones we want to keep and show. Chris also is training Real Gun babies owned by some of our customers."

Terry explained that she and Chris were attracted to Real Gun because of the quality of his sire, Playgun. She said they like his substance and the intensity he shows with cows. Playgun, a money-earner of repute, is an all-time leading cutting horse sire, as well as a National Reining Horse Association leading sire and a leading reined cow horse

Given the number of irons in the fire, the day will be a busy one.

sire, whose progeny had earned more than $3 million dollars by 2007. Real Gun's dam, an exceptional producer, has 13 offspring that are money-earners and AQHA point-earners.

Chris, who is pragmatic about breeding stallions, said the ranch also owns some shares of outside syndicated stallions and utilizes other stallions in the program. "It's more economical for us. This way, we're not locked into one or two studs. It takes a long time to get your investment back on a stallion, if you ever do get it. It's really a gamble in many ways."

Managing for Wildlife

An increasingly important component of the Stuart Ranch income now comes from hunting, due to four watershed lakes on the property, as well as Cow Creek. This abundance of water in a relatively dry region provides ideal habitat for waterfowl.

"We're on the edge of the eastern flyway," explained Terry, "and we have hundreds of thousands of geese on the ranch each year, as well as thousands of ducks. We're working to improve our hunting program as another, nonconflicting, source of revenue."

The ranch also has a healthy deer population and the ever-present scourge of the South—wild hogs. Hunters are eager to pursue bucks, which many ranchers now manage for large horn growth, and wild hogs can be hunted year-round, which extends

Unfortunately, not all the cattle work can be done horseback, although cowboys often alternate ground and riding jobs throughout the day.

As does any top ranch crew, the Stuart cowboys operate as if each is part of a well-oiled machine when it's branding time.

149

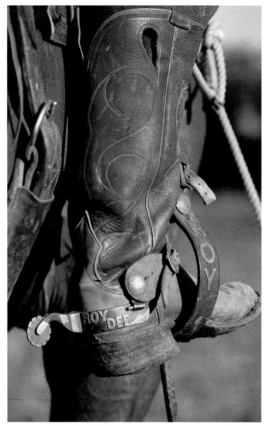

There is no doubt about who owns these spurs and stirrups. Cowboys frequently personalize their gear in such ways.

hunting revenue. Dove hunting also is popular in this area of the country.

Terry's youngest son, Robert, is especially interested in the hunting aspect of the ranch. He plans to study wildlife biology in college and apply what he learns to improve the Stuart Ranch hunting program.

"We've made conscious decisions to manage this ranch for both cattle and wildlife, and the two can actually complement each other," Terry said.

In the Future

Terry is very aware that, in order to survive, this long-established family ranch must remain profitable. As do all parents, she wants what is best for her sons and will support them in whatever they chose to do after college. But, if one or both choose to work on the ranch, she would be happy.

"They certainly understand what it takes to make a living here," she said. "They've spent a lot of holidays taking care of animals and missing things that were more fun."

It takes such day-to-day experience, as well as common sense and sometimes sheer luck,

A timeless tradition—ranch horses are hobbled in open country until it is time to go back to work.

This unique chap style is appropriate for the Oklahoma heat and ranch work, given the ring fastened to the top concha and chap pocket.

Stuart Ranch Timeline

1868: Robert Clay Freeny filed claim on what became known as Freeny Valley, and his "CF" brand was the first registered in the Oklahoma Indian Territory.

1880: Robert Terry Stuart was born near Lawrence, Texas.

1916: R.T. Stuart moved his insurance company headquarters to Oklahoma.

1931: R.T. Stuart married Ida Freeny, who inherited her family homestead, and together they built the Stuart Ranch, using the "Bar S" brand.

1949: Son R.T. "Bob" Stuart Jr., who followed his father's footsteps into the insurance and ranching industries, purchased Big Shot Dun from the Waggoner Ranch. Bob Stuart also changed the brand to the "7S."

1961: Miss T Stuart, an outstanding ranch broodmare was born. She produced top horses, and her daughters likewise produced excellent performance horses.

1963: Stuart Ranch purchased Son O Leo from fellow Oklahoman Bud Warren. Son O Leo sired 243 Stuart Ranch horses during the next 22 years.

1991: Bob Stuart asked his daughter, Terry Stuart Forst, to manage Stuart Ranch, a family corporation, initially to revitalize the ranch's cattle operation and, later, to improve the horse program, as well.

1995: Stuart Ranch received the Best Remuda Award from the American Quarter Horse Association and Bayer Animal Health. Stuart Ranch horse Genuine Redbud, a granddaughter of Miss T Stuart, won the AQHA Superhorse title.

1999: Texan Chris Littlefield, an accomplished horseman, joined the Stuart Ranch.

2002: Seven S Genuine Miss became the first AQHA high-point ranch-versatility award-winner.

2004: Real Gun earned the AQHA Superhorse title, as well as a National Reined Cow Horse Association bridle-horse world championship in the limited-open division.

to successfully run a ranch today. Certainly easier and more lucrative careers can lure the next generation away from the land. Ranching, however, is not so much an economic decision as it is a lifestyle choice. Working with the land and livestock, and successfully managing the vagaries of weather and markets, is deeply satisfying. But unlike many occupations, a rancher's work never is really done. Plus, for an outfit as deeply rooted in family ties as the Stuart Ranch, there is a sense of obligation in carrying on the tradition.

"I hope my sons and I can stand the test of time in the future, as the family has done in the past," Terry shared. "This ranch meant a lot to my dad and means a lot to us. I want to do everything I can to see that it stays in our family."

"We rode every day through the cattle and, as the snow and ice melted, we found more dead cattle in the canyons. It was one of the most heart-wrenching sights we'd ever seen."
Kim Crago

9

CRAGO RANCHES

Guy de Galard

O n a hot August afternoon, Bruce and Kim Crago pushed cattle across a rolling, golden South Dakota pasture. Son Colby had loped ahead to open the gate leading to the adjoining pasture and its water reservoir.

"Water is a big factor around here. This country relies on reservoirs and dams. Because of the changing weather pattern, and also because of the faster pace of life involving ranch management, phone calls and such that make time so valuable, ranching is not what it used to be," Bruce explained.

From Mining to Ranching

"What it used to be" started for the Cragos in 1870s England

Bruce and Kim Crago work together checking cattle, and when time allows, both compete in team roping.

153

Kim Crago participates in daily operations on the ranch and, when time allows, enjoys competing in ranch horse and working cow horse events.

when 15-year-old Peter Crago and his family embarked on a ship bound for America. Peter's final destination was the Michigan iron mines, where his uncle already was working. The 30-to-40-day ocean voyage was hard. There was no electricity aboard ship, and the only food available was dry bread.

"Once in awhile, they would put a little water on the bread to soften it up a bit," said Vince Crago, Peter's grandson.

After reaching America, as soon as Peter had enough money, he sent for his brother, Tom, and was able to send for his father, John Henry, a year later. However, John Henry, who longed for his homeland and the rest of his family, eventually returned to England, leaving his two sons to make it in America.

After about six years of working the iron mines, the two brothers, Peter and Tom, heard about the 1876 gold rush in the Black Hills. They wasted no time, and bought train tickets to the end of the line in Bismarck, N.D. From there, they joined a wagon train and, after walking most of the way, an average of eight miles a day, arrived in Deadwood 40 days later.

"About every day Indians would take a run at them, but they never did attack them [the wagon train]," Vince related. "They [the

Chuck Crago is shown with CM Dynamite Frost, a 1998 stallion by Do O Dynamite and out of Sierra Frost.

Indians] would get just out of rifle range, and they would whoop and holler, and go back and send up smoke signals. They never did bother them [the wagon train], just kind of scared them, I guess."

After only a short time in Deadwood, the two brothers soon realized that gold mining was not their calling.

"Grandpa told us he couldn't tell the difference between gold and fool's gold," Vince explained.

Before long, the brothers found themselves working for another mining company in Terraville. Unfortunately, the long working hours and rough living conditions took their toll on Tom, who died from diphtheria in 1879.

Peter soon found lodging in a boarding house, where he met his wife, Mary Ann Thompson of Galena, Ill. After her brother was killed in a Deadwood mining accident, Mary Ann persuaded Peter to change his occupation and start farming, a less dangerous activity.

In 1887, after leasing a farm for a few years, Peter purchased a parcel of farmland for $600. There he built a log home, where his family would live until the current house was built in 1933. After purchasing their 320 acres

Bruce Crago believes wet saddle blankets and many miles working cattle in rough country really put a horse to the test.

When a colt settles down, Colby Crago rewards the colt with a rub on the neck.

of land, Peter and Mary Ann planted 1,000 apple trees. The fruit was hauled to market and sold to the Deadwood and Lead miners.

"Ag people were broke at that time, and it was the miners who had the money," Vince recalled. "The orchard is what kept the family alive."

According to family legend, Vince's grandfather, Peter, spent long hours at the market, but never had to worry about staying too late. His team of horses knew the way home, so he could sleep on the way.

Vince's father, Charles, was born to Mary Ann and Peter in 1893. An avid horseman and cattleman without much interest in orchards, Charles eventually purchased the Crago homestead from his parents in the late 1920s, and started breeding and training work and ranch horses.

"When I was growing up during the 1930s and '40s, there was a great demand for broke saddle horses and for good teams. Somebody would come along and want to buy them," recalled Vince, who carried on the family tradition of ranching and raising fine horses.

Continuing the Legacy

Vince Crago was born May 9, 1926. After graduating from high school in 1944, he ranched in a family partnership with Charles, his father, and brothers. In 1951, he married Margaret Beckwith, and they had three sons—Bruce, Ralph and Chuck.

Since beef was Vince's business, he supported and promoted the industry however he could. He soon became involved with organizations, such as the South Dakota Stockgrowers Association, South Dakota Beef Council and the American National Cattlemen's Association.

"Since cattle were our livelihood, we felt it was important to give back," Vince once said. Margaret gave back to the industry that supported her family, as well, and was elected president of the South Dakota Cowbelles in 1972. But the family matriarch does not ride horses at all.

"A runaway team killed my grandfather. That always left an impression on me, and I was afraid of horses," she explained.

Range management also became an important aspect of Vince's ranching operation, and he always strived to be a good steward of the land. During his term as Lawrence County Farm Bureau president, he was instrumental in organizing and conducting educational tours for the organization's members. For his effort in promoting the

Crago mares earn the privilege of joining the ranch's broodmare band.

When halter-breaking a colt, Bruce Crago rewards every "try," or effort, a young horse makes to respond appropriately.

The Crago Ranch crew routinely moves cattle across the South Dakota grasslands.

159

Duns and buckskins are a legacy from such stallions as Beckwith Dun, Beckwith Playboy, Butte County Playboy, PC Bronsin and CM Dynamite Frost.

beef industry through the years, Vince was honored in January 2001 as the Stockman of the Year at the Black Hills Stock Show and Rodeo in Rapid City, S.D.

Eventually, Vince's partnership with his brothers was dissolved, and a new one formed with his sons and their families. Through the years, Vince and Margaret gradually turned over the ranch business to their sons and daughters-in-law—Bruce and Kim, Chuck and Mary, and Ralph and Becky. All have settled in the Belle Fourche area to continue the ranching tradition with their families, and Vince was able to pass on his passion for the cattle business and horses. Today, his children and grandchildren proudly carry on his work, and the Crago name has become synonymous with award-winning Quarter Horses.

On Aug. 4, 2006, Vince passed away after a lengthy battle with pancreatic cancer. Throughout his illness, however, he continued to enjoy his grandchildren and great-grandchildren participating in their various activities and ranch work. Vince also enjoyed watching his sons work cattle, even though he was too weak to help at times. A digni-

fied and kind man, Vince left a lasting legacy to his family and friends, as well as to the beef and horse industries. Most of all, he cherished every moment he spent with his wife, Margaret. Everyone in the family agrees that she was his "shining light."

Margaret still lives on the ranch where Vince was born. It has been in the Crago family for 120 years and was recognized in 1987 as a "Century Farm" by the South Dakota Historical Society.

Today the Crago Ranches are run individually by Bruce and wife Kim, Ralph and wife Becky, and Chuck and wife Mary. As their families have grown, the Crago sons have expanded their individual ranching operations to include the next generation. Their outfits encompass 70,000 deeded and leased acres, and family members work together to ensure that the Crago outfit and its traditions thrive.

"Besides having our own places, we are all partners and help out each other," Bruce said simply.

Each year, at the end of May, the ranches brand 1,200 to 1,400 head of calves. All family members are top hands and operate with the efficiency of people accustomed to working together as they rope, drag and wrestle calves. When the branding is complete, most of the livestock are trailed or trucked to summer grass range.

Then it is time to ready hay equipment for the fields. Becky and Ralph usually put up two cuttings of alfalfa from flood-irrigated fields. In late fall, the ranchers bring all the livestock back home, where they feed hay through the winter. Springtime finds everyone busy again, calving and foaling mares—even lambing at Ralph and Becky's ranch, where sheep are raised and yearling cattle have been fed through the winter.

Crago Ranch Horses

Vince purchased his first registered Quarter Horses in 1958 from Harley Roth. Since then, the ranch's Quarter Horse program has been built on the theory that all horses should have the "ranch-born" foundation, or be ranch-raised.

Vince was proud of the horses the family raises, rides, trains and uses on the ranch. Mares are pasture-bred and foal in open pastures. Early on, the foals develop stamina and good, tough feet, and learn how to travel in the rough country. The foals also usually share their pastures with cattle, which develops the young horses' natural cow sense.

The Crago family's primary goals have been to raise and offer solid ranch and performance horses that most everyone can get along with. The family believes in wet saddle blankets and many miles of working cattle through rough terrain to really put a horse to the test. The ranch-raised young horses, started outside, are given 30 days riding before the youngsters learn cattle-working basics and start earning their keep. By the time the horses are 4 years old, they are routinely used to gather cattle, rope cattle for doctoring and drag calves for branding. Today, the Crago Ranch owns a total of 160 horses, including 10 stallions and 60 ranch and performance horses.

"Raising cattle has really been the reason for our Quarter Horse program," said Kim, Vince's daughter-in-law who also competes in ranch horse and working cow horse events. "Here is where we feel the true ranch horse is trained, and the beginning of a potentially great performance horse is molded. A good ranch horse usually will make a good performance horse, and there is a better chance to have a winner if the horse has a good pedigree."

Family patriarch Vince Crago is shown here on Beckwith Dun, a cornerstone of the family's horse-breeding program.

Ralph Crago and "Trigger" were at a branding when this shot was taken.

*Riders
pushed cattle
toward the
branding
corral on
the Crago
Ranch.*

That certainly has held true for the Crago family competitors. Bruce, for example, began riding and competing on Quarter Horses at an early age and later won the 1986 Center of the Nation Quarter Horse Association Working Cow Horse Futurity. Brothers Bruce, Ralph and Chuck placed fourth in team penning at the 1991 American Quarter Horse Association World Championship Show. The three brothers were riding three geldings, half-brothers, all sired by Beckwith Dun. In the early 1990s, Bruce, brother Chuck and his wife, Mary, partnered to earn an AQHA reserve world championship in team penning. The South Dakota Rodeo Association has included team-penning competition on its slate of events, as well, and the three Crago brothers have won the SDRA championship for three years. Obviously willing dispositions and versatility are most important components for the Cragos' ranch-raised horses.

"Good, honest, broke horses are more difficult to find," Kim explained. "The mare's disposition is crucial to the development of the foal's attitude and trainability. We have narrowed our broodmares down to the ones that we feel have earned a right to be broodmares, first by their disposition and then by their own performances, and if they have pro-

duced colts that are being ridden and have been proven. Most of our mares have been ridden. The ones that haven't been ridden have sires or dams, brothers or sisters, or sons or daughters that have performance records."

Although the ranching family firmly believes in proven equine bloodlines, the Cragos also breed horses with versatility in mind. Chuck's wife, Mary, for example, promotes Crago horses for barrel racing.

"We don't breed for a specific event; therefore, we offer a very wide selection of bloodlines," Chuck said. "Although we have been upgrading our horse program every year, the market has become so competitive that we need to have the whole package."

Crago Ranch Stallions

Born in the Cheyenne River breaks north of Midland, S.D., Beckwith Dun has been a cornerstone of the Cragos' horse breeding program. The 1973 stallion was purchased as a 3-year-old in 1976 from Ralph Beckwith, Margaret Crago's father, and Vince, Bruce, Ralph and Chuck used the stallion to breed to their ranch mares. Beckwith Dun stamped his foals with his conformation, athletic ability and natural cow sense. Many of his get won halter futurities as weanlings and went on to win working cow horse futurities, as

Crago cattle quench their thirst in one of the ranch's reservoirs. "This country relies on reservoirs and dams," Bruce Crago stressed.

well as team roping, barrel racing and team penning events.

Today, Beckwith Playboy, a 1992 dun stallion by Beckwith Dun and out of Miss Playboy, continues the tradition of siring eye-catching, working-bred horses with conformation, color and cow sense.

"The goal of our breeding is simple: We attempt to breed a versatile horse that would meet the needs of the ranch and that we personally would use for doctoring, branding and sorting livestock," Ralph stated. "We believe that by taking proven foundation bloodlines, like the Beckwith Duns, and interspersing some modern and popular cow-working bloodlines, a breeder can raise a remarkable Quarter Horse with conformation, athletic ability, natural cow sense and a good disposition."

One good example of such a horse is Butte County Playboy, a 1998 dun stallion by Beckwith Playboy and out Zhura Star, a foundation-bred mare. An AQHA point-earner in reining and working cow horse, a South Dakota Reined Cow Horse Association money-earner, and 2004 Central States Fair ladies ranch horse champion, the stallion has proven his versatility in the arena and on the ranch.

PC Bronsin also has been instrumental in establishing the reputation of Crago horses for many years. The 1985 buckskin stallion, by Sun Frost and out of Red Rockette, still perfectly sound, has sired every color foal possible. At the 2000 World Foundation Quarter Horse Alliance Show in Denver, Colo., PC Bronsin earned reserve high-point honors. In 2000 and 2001, Chuck won the Black Hills Stock Show ranch horse competitions on "Rainy," by PC Bronsin, and also earned reserve honors at the Gillette, Wyo., winter show.

Equally outstanding among the Cragos' stallion battery is CM Dynamite Frost, a 1998 buckskin Doc O Dynamite stallion out of Sierra Frost, a half-sister to "Bozo," Kristie Peterson's world champion barrel horse. In 2001, CM Dynamite Frost won second in the South Dakota Reined Cow Horse Association Breeders open division and was a finalist at the Wyoming Reined Cow Horse Association Futurity, as well.

Currently, the ranch stands three additional stallions that further contribute to the ranch's reputation for solid performance horses in arenas across the country. One is

The "rocking chair" is one of the Crago's horse brands.

CM Nonstop Charlie, by the now-deceased Nonstop Bubblin and out of San Crystalita. By Nonstop Jet, Nonstop Bubblin and Mary Crago won the 2001 Women's Professional Rodeo Association Divisional Tour Badlands Circuit championship.

In January 2005, Duals Blue Peppy arrived at the ranch. The 2003 bay roan stallion is by National Cutting Horse Association money-earner Duals Blue Boon and out of Sweet Peppy Again, a daughter of Peppy San Badger. Chuck Crago and Duals Blue Peppy recently won the breeders' non-pro division of the South Dakota Reined Cow Horse Association Futurity.

Sabre Blue Gun, a 2003 gray stallion, is by Blue Boy Doc, by Docs Prescription, and out of Wares May Gun, a granddaughter of Dry Doc on the top and a great-granddaughter of Doc's Lynx on the bottom. Blue Boy Doc not only is

This barn, built in 1920, is on Ralph and Becky Crago's property.

an NCHA money-earner and sire of NCHA and National Reining Horse Association winners, but also sired Apache Blue Boy, a three-time AQHA world champion heeling horse. Ralph and Becky's daughter, Kristy, will promote Sabre Blue Gun in roping horse futurities and ranch horse competitions.

"Our program is built around these famous, versatile foundation sires," Chuck commented.

Crago Cattle

Belle Fourche's history is directly linked to that of South Dakota's cattle industry, which developed there in the 1870s and '80s. The city was named by French explorers when France owned the region for the confluence of what are now known as the Belle Fourche and Redwater Rivers and the Hay Creek. Beaver trappers worked these rivers until the mid-1800s, and Belle Fourche became a well-known fur-trading rendezvous point.

During the 1876 gold rush in the nearby Black Hills, the open plains for hundred of miles in all directions were filled by huge cattle herds coming from Texas and Kansas. Towns sprang up to serve the farmers' and ranchers' ever-changing needs.

In 1884, the Marquis de Mores, a French nobleman and contemporary of Theodore Roosevelt, established a stage line between Medora, N.D., and Deadwood, S.D. The Belle Fourche way station included a stage barn and a saloon. By 1890, the first trainload of cattle had headed east. By 1895, Belle Fourche was shipping 2,500 carloads of cattle per month in the peak season, making it the world's largest livestock shipping point. This is the era portrayed in the 1972 John Wayne movie *The Cowboys*, which describes a cattle drive from Montana to Belle Fourche. The town is also known as the geographic center of the nation.

Today the Cragos carry on the region's cattle-ranching tradition, running 1,400 mother cows and 400 to 500 yearlings annually. In 1976, after attending a seminar in Fort Robinson, Neb., Vince expanded the cattle operation with a crossbreeding program between Hereford cows and Angus bulls, thus improving the quality and weight of the calves. One of the first area ranchers to add crossbreeding to his cow-calf operation, Vince believed in brands and brand inspections as proof of a rancher's livestock ownership. The ranch also used Longhorns for easy heifer calving and maintained 80 Longhorns cows until the late 1990s.

Unforgiving Weather

Although the Belle Fourche area is known as prime cattle country, winters there can be harsh and unforgiving. Kim recalled one of the worst such winter setbacks the Crago family has experienced:

"The spring blizzard of 1997 was one of the worst storms in South Dakota history. It also was a terrible disaster for the cattle. The day before the storm hit, the weather was absolutely beautiful—75 degrees. Baby calves were bucking and playing in the warm sunshine. The ranch was in the prime of calving, as we usually start calving around March 25th, and by the first week of April, many calves already had been born.

"The weatherman predicted a strong storm with wind and rain, nothing too serious. It was supposed to be over in a day or so, and temperatures would warm back up. Everyone knew that rain and wind can be tough on baby calves, so we prepared to get the cattle situated to weather the small storm the best we could.

"By evening, the rain had moved in, and the wind was blowing. It continued to gain speed, and the temperatures dropped to the teens. The rain changed to ice and then snow. Wind speeds were clocked at more than 80 miles per hour. The weather report said that the storm had circled back into itself, some-

what like a hurricane does, and that it would be much worse than predicted.

"We paced the floor all night long, wondering what the next day would bring. The storm turned into a full-fledged blizzard by daylight. We could hardly see, but tried to make our way horseback to the cattle. After riding a short distance from the barn, we knew it was too dangerous to ride in the storm.

"Then we got into pickups and drove to the pastures, to try and save any calves we could find. We could barely see through the wind-driven, icy snow. We found several [calves], some under snow, some just lying on the prairie, iced over. We gathered several and hauled them to the house. A few survived, but many were lost.

"This was at just one ranch. The majority of the cow herd was 17 miles away on another ranch that had deep canyons and gullies, with a lot of protection, which, we thought, would keep most of the cattle safe. But the wind, sleet and snow proved us wrong. The guys had tried to get to the cattle, but the depth of the snow and the reduced visibility had shut down the major highway to the ranch.

"We sat it out for another day, as we took care of the calves at our individual ranches.

A wagon wheel adds a touch of western décor on the ranch.

Two ranch brands are on the sign in Vince and Margaret Crago's yard.

When the storm finally cleared, we headed to the ranch with the big herd of cows. We could not believe what we found.

"We rode to a set of corrals, where we could see some cows lying down, resting, like normal. When we got to them, they were actually dead, frozen solid, in an upright position with their heads up. We knew from that point on, it would be a horrific sight as we started searching for cows and calves. We would ride over a hill and see two or three calves sucking on one cow. There were dead cows and dead calves everywhere.

"The survivors were in terrible shape. The wind and sleet had literally knocked all of the hair off the cattle's hind ends, like a sandblaster, where they stood with their backs to the storm. They had bloody, frozen ears and tails, their bags were frozen and wind-burned. Some wouldn't let their calves suck because the cows were too sore; many were blinded and disorientated.

"We roped and doctored cows with sore bags, and tried to mother up the survivors for two weeks after the storm. We rode every day through the cattle and, as the snow and ice melted, we found more dead cattle in the canyons. It was one of the most heart-wrenching sights we'd ever seen."

A Look to the Future

Through good times and bad, the Crago family has survived. Bruce, Ralph and Chuck's children are the fifth generation to carry on the family ranching business. And just as they did, their children now are learning from their parents and grandparents to care for cattle and horses. As always, responsibility goes hand in hand with the ranching lifestyle, and the next generation of Cragos have learned to help whenever and wherever necessary to ensure the outfit's survival.

Through the years, an ever-increasing number of Crago cousins have become competitors, too. They understand well how to showcase the family's ranch-raised horses, and even the ranch cattle and sheep. All the cousins have competed successfully in 4-H, Little Britches and National High School Rodeo Association events, and most have gone on to compete in rodeos, ropings and ranch-horse competition. But no matter the sport, the focus

The Crago Ranch was homesteaded more than a century ago in South Dakota.

remains on the capable Crago Ranch horses, a legacy from prior generations.

Vince Crago's sons—Bruce, Chuck and Ralph—hope their children and grandchildren can continue to enjoy the family's traditional ranching lifestyle. As with many such outfits, operating costs continue to rise, and ensuring that the next generation can maintain the land for ranching is an ongoing consideration.

Nonetheless, as Kim Crago pointed out, "Ranching is still a great family business, and can continue to be when the generations work together as they do here on the Crago Ranches."

Crago Ranch Timeline

1870s: Fifteen-year-old Peter Crago and his family left England, bound for America and work in the Michigan iron mines.

1876: Peter and his brother, Tom, left the iron mines to join the 1876 gold rush in the Black Hills.

1887: Peter and wife Mary Ann Thompson purchased their first parcel of land, which soon developed into fruit orchards.

1893: Son Charles was born to Peter and Mary Ann Crago.

1926: Vince Crago, Charles' son, was born.

Late 1920s: Charles purchased the Crago homestead from his parents and changed the focus from apple orchards to breeding and training draft and ranch horses.

1944: After high school graduation, Vince became a partner in his family's ranching operation.

1951: Vince Crago married Margaret Beckwith, and the couple had three sons—Bruce, Chuck and Ralph, who later partnered with their father on the family ranch.

1958: Crago Ranch purchased its first registered Quarter horse.

1976: The Cragos purchased Beckwith Dun from Margaret Crago's father, and the stallion became a cornerstone of the ranch's horse program, as did PC Bronsin more than a decade later.

1987: The South Dakota Historical Society designated the Crago Ranch homestead a "Century Farm," recognizing the family's 100-plus years in the livestock industry.

2001: The Black Hills Stock Show and Rodeo in Rapid City, S.D., named Vince Crago Stockman of the Year.

2006: Vince Crago passed away, and his children and grandchildren continue to honor his ranching legacy.

"Our goal is to breed the world's best ranch horse, and despite our interest in racing and performance horses, that remains our focus."
Glenn Blodgett, DVM

10

FOUR SIXES RANCH

By Holly Endersby

The gleaming bronze replica of famous Quarter Horse stallion Dash for Cash—in full racing stride, jockey on his back—shimmers in the sunlight that infuses the statue with lifelike grace. Set amid a sea of lush green grass, in front of big red barns emblazoned with 6666, the statue honors the stallion whose get have earned more than $36 million. The bronze is a fitting greeting for visitors to the Burnett Ranches Ltd. Four Sixes Ranch in Guthrie, Texas.

Lining the long drive to the breeding barns, tidy fences border huge pastures filled with herds of gorgeous mares and playful foals. In springtime, a steady stream of pickups with horse trailers makes the pilgrimage to the ranch, long known

In addition to breeding top racing and performance horses, the Four Sixes remains focused on breeding hardy, cow-savvy ranch horses.

171

for its outstanding Quarter Horses. The Four Sixes is recognized not only as being among the West's premier cattle ranches, but also as unique among Quarter Horse breeding operations.

Breeding the Best

"We're the only Quarter Horse barn that breeds both racing and performance horses," stated the ranch's horse manager, Glenn Blodgett, DVM. "The current stallions standing at the Four Sixes represent some of the best bloodlines in the Quarter Horse industry."

Glenn should know. Since he was hired in 1982 by owner Anne Marion to improve the Four Sixes horse operation, several immaculate barns, a mare motel, outside pens and stallion facilities have been built, as well as

When horse manager Dr. Glenn Blodgett came to the ranch in 1982, his mission was to improve the Four Sixes' horse operation. He has.

a comfortable combination bunkhouse for veterinary interns and cookhouse for staff. Some fourth-year students do short externships here, alongside several yearlong interns. In addition, Glenn and his staff are equine veterinarians for the surrounding ranches and families, a service Burnett Ranches graciously provides. But breeding the best Quarter Horses is the main focus.

"We want to keep the best stallions standing at the ranch as part of our overall marketing strategy," Glenn said. "The best studs draw the best mares, either for artificial insemination or embryo transfer, which will continue to add value to our program."

The manager-veterinarian explained that even stallions not owned by the ranch usually stay there year-round. "That way, potential breeding-contract buyers can see the studs, as we always have someone on hand to show people around."

Simply called "Doc," the unassuming veterinarian in green, knee-high rubber boots and coveralls presides over an ultramodern clinic, where all records are computerized and immediately available. If an attending veterinarian wants to know any mare's fertility history, an assistant retrieves that information on a laptop computer and relates the history.

Speed and efficiency make breeding large numbers of mares possible, a critical factor at the Four Sixes. Glenn said the ranch breeds about 800 mares on-site and provides fresh, cooled and frozen semen for another 700 mares. In anybody's book, that's a lot of breeding.

"Our goal is to breed the world's best ranch horse," Glenn remarked, "and despite our interest in racing and performance horses, that remains our focus. If some make it as outstanding cutters, reiners or reined cow horses, that's great, but that's not our overriding goal."

Desirable Traits, Quality Bloodlines

Bloodlines within the ranch-breeding program contain the equine traits Glenn—and the working cowboys—think are important, such as the speed and agility of the modern cutting horse, but without sacrificing size. Each year, Glenn personally selects stallions for the ranch program.

"If someone says, 'That horse is too big,' it's usually one I want to go see," he said. "I don't want a huge horse, but I do need one with enough size and athletic ability to handle the cattle and stay sound."

Because of the long distances horses must travel on the rugged, nearly 300,000-acre ranch during high summer temperatures, staying power is essential.

"Stamina in a Four Sixes horse is extremely important," Glenn related. "That—along with good bone, defined withers, a short back with a long underline and deep heart girth, good feet, correct conformation, a nice hip to provide power behind, and short cannon bones and pasterns, which generally seem to yield a horse that is more athletic and smoother to ride—is what make a good ranch horse."

As with most ranches, the Four Sixes emphasizes broodmare quality. "The broodmares in the band have generations of breeding that back up what we are trying to produce," Glenn stated. "They are a solid foundation to work from. But we are careful to improve each generation while still maintaining a quality ranch horse."

Racing stallions in which the ranch owned shares and stood at stud recently include First N Kool, Ocean Runaway, Eyesa Special and Stoli, all descendents of Dash for Cash. The great racing stallion is still the all-time leading sire of racing Quarter Horses. Mr Jess Perry's race and stakes earnings of almost $700,000 put him in the upper echelons among running Quarter Horses. The ranch owns shares in the syndicated stallion, who also stands at stud there. As for performance stallions, the ranch owns Seven From Heaven, Playin Attraction and Sixes Pick outright, as well as shares in the syndicated and partnership stallions Paddys Irish Whiskey, Royal Fletch and Playin Stylish.

Quality horses have been part of the ranch legacy for many decades. Among the ranch's foundation stallions were Joe Hancock, an all-time great rope-horse sire; Grey Badger II, known for his speed and "legs of iron;" and Hollywood Gold, born in 1940 at the Iowa Park, Texas, Burnett ranch and former manager George Humphreys' favorite stallion.

Humphreys managed the ranch from 1932 to 1970 after coming to the ranch as a hand in 1918. He was hired by the first manager, Bud Arnett, who, in turn, had been selected by ranch founder Burk Burnett. Humphreys used Hollywood Gold, known for his good nature, for many years. The stallion's get went on to win cutting competitions nationwide.

The blood of Hollywood Gold and these notable foundation stallions still graces the lines of many current ranch geldings and broodmares.

A Dynasty is Born

Before the age of 20, Samuel Burk Burnett established himself as a major Texas cattleman. Born in Missouri in 1849, Burk, at age 10, had come to Denton County, Texas, with his parents, Jeremiah and Mary Burnett, and his father began running wild Longhorn cattle there.

As did most youngsters of the era, Burk grew up fast, caring for the family cattle while his father served in the Civil War. At age 19, young Burk bought his first 100 head of cattle in Denton County from Frank Crowley. The

Sixes Pick is all that his name implies. The stallion is considered the best son of Tanquery Gin, who strongly influenced the ranch-breeding program.

173

Reggie
Hatfield
waits for the
opportune
moment to
rope the
horse of
choice.

cattle wore the "6666" brand, which Burk recorded in Wichita County in 1875 and again on the Kiowa-Comanche Reservation in 1881. He continued filing the 6666 brand, destined to become one of the best known in the American West, in subsequent counties as his herds and land ownership expanded.

Burk began to amass his fortune by wintering cattle during the 1873 panic and selling them for a $10,000 profit the following spring. The next year, he bought 1,300 head in south Texas and drove them north along the Chisholm Trail to open-range grazing near the Little Wichita River. Although Burk's cattle grazed on open range, he quickly realized that the man who owned land had more control over his fortune, so he began a concentrated effort to buy top grazing land.

His first headquarters were near present-day Wichita Falls, Texas. But serious drought in the 1880s forced Burk and other area ranchers to find better grazing. They did so by negotiating a lease with the last great Comanche chief, Quanah Parker. The lease,

Through the years, the ranch's quality horses have drawn such cowboys as Boots O'Neal to ride for the brand.

Sixes cowboy Reggie Hatfield sorts through the horse herd.

175

covering an area of Indian Territory north of the Red River in Oklahoma, remained in effect until the early 1900s. During the lease period, Burk forged a lifelong friendship with Parker, and the two exchanged many gifts through the years. Many years later, Burk's great-great-granddaughter, Anne Marion, gave these priceless gifts from Quanah Parker and his wives to the National Ranching Heritage Center in Lubbock, Texas, where they remain for public enjoyment today.

Near the turn of the 20th century, Burk bought the 8 Ranch near Guthrie, Texas, from the Louisville Land and Cattle Company, and the Dixon Creek Ranch in the Texas Panhandle from the Cunard Line. Not only did these acquisitions provide the necessary

Red barns branded with the "Four Sixes" are an inherent part of the ranch's heritage.

grazing lands for his cattle, but by 1921 also provided enormous oil revenues. Burk next established the Four Sixes Ranch's new headquarters at the 8 Ranch site.

Burk and his first wife, Ruth B. Loyd, daughter of wealthy Fort Worth banker M.B. Loyd, married in 1869 and had three children, two of whom died. The couple later divorced, and Burk remarried in 1892, but the only child of that union died as well.

In 1917, despite maintaining a residence in Fort Worth, where his financial business was centered, Burk Burnett decided to build "the finest ranch house in West Texas." He hoped the house would be a fitting testimony to the cattle industry's importance in his adopted state, as well as a fine place to house the ranch manager and entertain such influential friends as Theodore Roosevelt and Will Rogers.

Built at a cost of $100,000, an astronomical sum in those days, and from rock quarried on the ranch, the enormous 11-bedroom house also showcased hunting trophies, Indian artifacts and beautiful art. Ironically, when the house was built, Burk continued to sleep most often about a mile down the road toward Guthrie, in the back room of the Four Sixes supply house, which stands to this day.

Subsequent Generations

At the time of his death in 1922, Burk had one surviving child, 51-year-old Tom Burnett. Previously, when Tom's grandfather, M. B. Loyd, had died in 1912, Tom already had received one-fourth of his Wichita County properties, as well as a substantial amount of money. Loyd, an avid race fan, as many wealthy Texans were at the time, had his own stable of fine horses, all branded with the single letter "L," and to this day Four Sixes horses still carry his brand on their left shoulder.

Despite family wealth, Tom learned ranching the hard way—as a hand on his father's spread. He started as a line rider at age 15, checking cattle on more than 50,000 acres on the Red River. At 21, Tom became wagon boss of the Indian Territory cattle operation and felt settled enough to marry Olive "Ollie" Lake of Fort Worth.

By the time he was 30, Tom had leased the old Wichita County Burnett lands from his father. And in 1920, Tom bought the 26,000-acre Triangle Ranch near Iowa Park, Texas, which remained in the family until the 1980s. Oil discovered there quickly increased Tom's already substantial fortune. In 1969, a major oil field was struck on the Four Sixes and continues contributing to the overall revenue flow.

Tom and Ollie had one child, a daughter, Anne Valiant Burnett, born in 1900. The couple later divorced, and despite marrying again, Tom had no other children. When he died in 1938, his estate went, intact, to his daughter, "Miss Anne," as she was known. Miss Anne already was custodian for the bulk of her grandfather Burk Burnett's estate, which, at the time of his death, he had put in trust for her yet unborn child.

Recognized for her knowledge of cattle and horses in particular, Miss Anne was a key supporter of the fledgling American Quarter Horse Association and was inducted into the Quarter Horse Hall of Fame in 1990. She was married to Jim Hall, with whom she had her daughter, Anne, and later, to Charles Tandy, who founded the Tandy Corporation. In 1978 Miss Anne established the Burnett Foundation to support a wide variety of activities ranging from horse racing to museums.

When Miss Anne died in 1980, the ranch and fortune passed to her daughter, Anne W. Marion, who sold the Triangle Ranch, but kept the Four Sixes and the Dixon Creek Ranches. Today she is sole owner of those outfits and takes an active interest in all aspects of their operation, and she, too, has one daughter and one granddaughter. Under Anne Marion's able leadership, the horse operation started and nourished by Miss Anne, her mother, has become quite influential in the Quarter Horse world.

The Breeding Business

Horse breeding is serious business at the Four Sixes. It is a priority not only for owner Anne Marion, but also a passion with veterinarian and horse manager Dr. Glenn Blodgett. The deceptively mild-mannered native Texan runs an impeccably managed breeding program on a scale few ranches would ever attempt.

"Breeding season is like a flat-topped pyramid with a rise beginning in February, a long flat top from March to May and a gradual decline to July," Glenn explained.

The first of April until the end of the first week of May is the peak season. By mid-May, most racing-bred mares have foaled

Each cowboy has a string of eight to 12 geldings, and he routinely rotates among them so that no one horse is ridden too hard.

Cowboys and horses make some big circles on the large ranch, no matter the season or weather.

and have been rebred. Twenty-four-hour human surveillance of these expensive, pregnant mares is essential, as most are bred on foal heats so their babies will arrive early in the year.

"The race mares are a little more fragile," Glenn commented, "so they all foal in stalls. They're used to more controlled environments and are apt to have more problems than ranch mares."

Performance mares not owned by the ranch typically foal prior to their arrival at the ranch for breeding. Ranch mares foal outside, and they experience few problems. The sheer number of foals is mind-boggling.

"We foal out about 300 babies a year," Glenn said in a matter-of-fact way.

Embryo transfer is a growing part of the ranch-breeding program. Veterinarians typically harvest two to four embryos from each of the high-value mares at the ranch for that

This gray obviously has the physical substance required to do a day's work, an asset shared by all the horses in the ranch remuda.

Turnout is an essential part of the ranch-horse routine at the Sixes.

Sixes cowboys continue to live their traditional lifestyle going into the 21ˢᵗ century.

purpose. On-site recipient mares add significantly to the ranch's overall horse population.

"Embryo transfer has been good for business," stated Glenn. "The owners are able to sell more breedings, which bring in additional revenue. And we're able to sell more breedings to people doing embryo transfer elsewhere, as well."

Currently, more embryo transfers are done with racing-bred mares, although Glenn also sees an upturn in performance-horse transfers. "In areas like Weatherford, Texas, where cutting is really hot, you'll find plenty of veterinary practices doing embryo transfers. It also adds considerable value to a mare because she can produce many more offspring."

Influential Stallions

Selecting stallions is a critical part of the Four Sixes horse program. Glenn carries that responsibility and has a history of picking winners.

"The racing stallions, Dash for Cash, Streakin Six and Special Effort, have proven to be excellent studs for us," he affirmed.

Dash for Cash was 23 years old when he was humanely euthanized May 20, 1996, following a bout with equine protozoal myeloencephalitis, which caused a loss of

Ranch broodmares typically foal outside and experience few problems.

180

hind-leg coordination. Dash for Cash's ashes are buried at the American Quarter Horse Heritage Center and Museum in Amarillo, near another statue of him there.

Special Effort, who joined the ranch in 1993, is the only racing Quarter Horse triple-crown winner at Ruidoso Downs, given his wins at the Ruidoso, Rainbow and All American Futurities. Retired to stud in 1982, Special Effort won 13 races out of 14 starts.

As for performance and ranch horses, Glenn thinks Tanquery Gin has most influenced the ranch-breeding program. A noted cutting and reining horse sire, Tanquery Gin carried the rich performance blood of Doc O'Lena, Doc Bar, Three Bars, Poco Bueno, Pretty Boy and King.

"We're going to feel his influence for a long time," Glenn predicted. "Unlike Gray Badger II, Joe Hancock and Hollywood Gold, all of whom were outstanding stallions, Tanquery Gin lived a long life. We were able to maximize his influence with the use of artificial insemination, which wasn't available with the earlier studs."

According to Glenn, Tanquery Gin possessed all the traits the outfit wanted in any ranch stallion. Luckily, the Four Sixes has a number of his daughters in the broodmare band, plus what Glenn considers to be his best son, Sixes Pick.

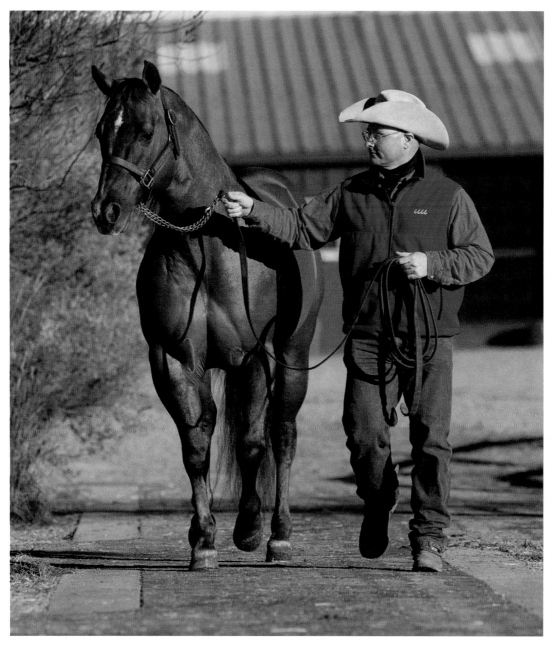

Mr Sun O Lena, a son of the great Doc O'Lena, stands at the Sixes.

"Sixes Pick also is going to have a lot of influence on our ranch herd," Glenn predicted. "He's a good-looking horse with excellent speed and a lot of endurance."

The ranch uses the latest breeding techniques to expand the stallions' influence through time and space. "We're freezing semen on the current studs," reported Glenn. "It can last indefinitely if stored properly. With frozen semen we're tapping foreign markets we've not been able to before."

Guthrie residents, no doubt, are accustomed to seeing horses from the Sixes being herded along area roadways.

Ranch cow-horse semen is most popular in Australia, and racing semen sells most frequently to Brazil. Reining horse semen most often goes to Europe, where the sport's popularity is rapidly growing.

Horse Promotion and Sales

Between racing and performance horses, the ranch sells about 150 head a year. As for racing Quarter Horses, long-established sales focus predominately on yearlings, although broodmares are sold, as well. Performance horses are sold at ranch-production and select sales, and at private treaty.

To boost the ranch-horse program's profile, some horses are shown, typically in Ranch Horse Association of America competitions, where cowboys compete on horses they believe best represent the ranch. The ranch pays all fees and costs, and the men keep any winnings. Resident trainer Chance O'Neal, son of Joe O'Neal of the Waggoner Ranch, starts most of the colts. Boyd Rice is the off-ranch trainer.

"Competition gets the ranch horse out in the public more and establishes a verifiable show record that helps promote and sell our

The horse herd has ample room to roam on the Texas ranch's wide-open spaces.

horses," explained Glenn. "So we want to be sure what the men show will reflect well on the ranch."

Cattle and Cowboys

As with most Texas ranches, cattle founded the Burnett family empire. Although oil has played a significant role since then, the ranch's historical commitment to raising quality cattle remains to this day.

The Four Sixes' cattle empire began when Burk Burnett gathered wild Longhorn cattle off the south Texas range and drove them north to sell. In 1868, he had purchased cattle branded with "6666," a difficult brand to modify, and bought the right to use that brand, which cattle on the Four Sixes Ranch still carry today.

Compared to European breeds, the native Texas Longhorns were rangy cattle, built more for survival than for beef production. To improve his herd, Burnett introduced purebred Herefords as herd sires and as heifers. Such crossbreeding produced a hardy animal that produced more beef.

However, further crossbreeding continued to improve the herd. Former manager J.J. Gibson crossed the ranch cows with Brangus bulls, themselves a cross between Brahma and Angus cattle. These bulls increased the herd's adaptability to the ranch's rough terrain, and were used until 1996, when they were replaced with Angus bulls. J.J.'s son, current manager Mike Gibson is phasing out the Hereford cow base. To match market demand, the ranch is moving to strictly Angus cows.

Today, with 7,500 mother cows and 450 Angus bulls, all worked by seven cowboys horseback, the Four Sixes hasn't strayed from its original ranching roots. During weaning and branding, Mike, who has a Texas Tech degree in agricultural economics, doubles the crew with seasonal riders.

To cover the vast territory and manage cattle well, cowboys are distributed around the ranch. Some live at camps, where each man is responsible for the animals and area nearest him. Others live at headquarters, and their assignments vary.

Although the Four Sixes historically was a Hereford ranch, the outfit has now transitioned to Black Angus in response to market preference. All cattle are marketed as yearlings, run through feedlots and sold to large meat-processing plants.

Sorting cattle is just another day's work for a Sixes horse, and many now demonstrate such skills in cutting, cow-horse and ranch-horse competition.

In recent years Angus bulls have replaced the Brangus bulls that were used to improve the herd's ability to adapt to the rough terrain.

183

The Sixes' Supply House, built about 1900, remains in use today and serves both ranch employees and the public.

The Sixes is a traditional outfit in that a horseback cowboy remains a valued employee when cattle are penned and worked.

Mike has sole responsibility for selecting replacement heifers from ranch herds, as well as the bulls typically purchased from breeders the ranch has done business with for years.

"Like most large ranches today, we age and source-verify all our cattle," Mike said. "We keep about 900 heifers and pick up around 150 bulls each year. We want good, deep-bodied bulls for this rugged country. I want to be sure they have the structure and size we need, so I select each one personally."

The Essential Remuda

At headquarters each morning, a cowboy jingles the horses into a corral, where each man selects two or three head apiece for the day. The remaining horses are turned onto pasture, and the day's mounts are loaded into trailers and driven to the ranch sections the cowboys will ride. Horses are rotated regularly, so no one horse is ridden too hard.

"Turnout is essential," Glenn stated. "We have very little sickness among the remuda because the horses get a healthy combination of work, rest and a natural environment."

According to Mike, each cowboy has his string of eight to 12 geldings, including a couple of young horses.

"There's been a big change in the way we start the colts. We use the Ray Hunt method, and it makes a much gentler horse. We don't have those old wild, tough horses anymore," Mike said.

With pastures thousands of acres in size, cowboys prefer horses with smooth gaits, especially the trot, the most used gait of all. In addition, agility and stamina are essential.

"We wean [cattle] in June when temperatures can be more than 100 degrees," said Glenn. "The cowboys have to be mounted on horses that can handle that."

The horses also must naturally want to work cattle, or they don't stay long on the ranch. Staying with tradition, the Four Sixes cowboys still drag calves to the fire.

"We brand by pastures," Mike explained. "The calves are mostly born in October, and we brand during February and March."

Reclaiming Grazing Land

One of the biggest changes during the past 40 years: The ranch has successfully reclaimed pastureland from invasive red berry juniper and mesquite.

"When my dad came here in 1970, the brush was terrible," Mike recalled.

Before the region was settled, wildfire played a significant role in keeping rangeland open. But when ranchers arrived, they began putting out most fires, which allowed juniper and mesquite to literally take over thousands of square miles of valuable Texas range. Now, the pendulum has swung back. The ranch has a fulltime brush crew, attacking the undesirable, invasive plants by spraying, burning, chaining and grubbing them from the pasturelands.

"I'm a big controlled-burn fan," Mike stated. "Depending on the rainfall, we burn significant parts of the ranch every year to control brush. When my grandfather settled here, it was mostly open grassland due to fire. We're trying to return the land to its more native state, and we're making good progress."

Longevity and Stability

Because Mike's father, J.J., was manager before him for 21 years, Mike has literally grown up on the Four Sixes. Longevity among

A bronze of the immortal Dash For Cash greets visitors to the Four Sixes Ranch in Guthrie, Texas.

185

The Four Sixes foals out approximately 300 babies annually.

Road signs are not a bad idea on an outfit the size of this Texas ranch.

Four Sixes Timeline

1868: Burk Burnett, at age 19, bought his first 100 head of cattle, all wearing the "6666" brand, which remains in use today.

1869: Burk married his first wife, Ruth B. Loyd. Their only surviving child, Tom, later ran the family business.

1873-1874: During the 1873 panic, Burk profitably wintered cattle and purchased more, grazing them on open range.

1880s- early 1900s: Following lease negotiations with Comanche chief Quanah Parker, Burk and other ranchers grazed their cattle on Oklahoma Indian Territory range.

1900: "Miss Anne" Valiant Burnett, Tom's only child, was born.

1917: Burk built "the finest ranch house in West Texas," an 11-bedroom showplace costing the then-astronomical sum of $100,000.

1920: Tom Burnett, Burk's son, bought the 26,000-acre Triangle Ranch near Iowa Park, Texas, which remained a family holding until the 1980s.

1921: Burk's previously purchased 8 Ranch and Dixon Creek Ranch began producing oil, and the Four Sixes' new headquarters soon were established on the 8 Ranch.

1922: Burk Burnett died, and granddaughter Anne Valiant Burnett became custodian for the bulk of the estate, which was to be passed to her as-yet unborn child.

1938: Tom Burnett died and his estate went to his daughter, Miss Anne.

1969: A major oil field was discovered on the Four Sixes.

1980: Miss Anne died, and her daughter, Anne W. Marion, later sold the Triangle Ranch, but kept the Four Sixes and Dixon Creek Ranches.

1982: Glenn Blodgett, DVM, was hired as the ranch's horse manager and to improve the Four Sixes horse operation.

1990: Miss Anne was inducted into the American Quarter Horse Association's Hall of Fame.

1993: The Four Sixes received the American Quarter Horse Association's Remuda Award for producing top ranch horses.

its managers' and hands' tenures creates stability in the ranch community. On a ranch this large, wives, as well as their cowboy husbands, often find employment. Ranch wives can be found in such places as division offices and the huge breeding facility.

"We're local boys," Mike explained. "My grandfather was an early settler, and our family ranch is next to the Four Sixes. Most of the guys working for me have been here for double-digit years. The only vacancies we get are from retirements or promotions."

When he does get to hire someone, Mike knows whom he wants: "I want a good, settled family man. If a guy is a good family man, he'll most often make a good ranch hand."

According to Mike, a family man benefits the local community of Guthrie, too. As do many rural communities today, Guthrie depends on the nearby large ranches for its social and community infrastructure, including the school.

Mike proudly explained why longtime employees make up the Sixes' work force. "The ranch always has been a leader in benefits for cowboys and other employees, and the owners have always been generous. We are provided with health insurance, retirement plans and housing."

One other aspect of the Four Sixes makes it unique among many large ranches today: The owner is an active member of the ranch team.

"Mrs. Marion is very involved," Mike stressed. "She's a real hands-on owner and comes to the ranch frequently."

Today, despite such modern conveniences as cell phones, computers and sophisticated breeding techniques, one thing remains the same on the Four Sixes—dedication to a lifestyle most Americans can no longer experience.

"Raising cattle is hard work," Mike said. "But for a cowboy, it's a lifestyle choice. And on the Four Sixes, that's a very good life."

"Two words that define the Pitchfork are 'tradition' and 'consistency.'"
James Gholson

11

PITCHFORK LAND & CATTLE CO.

By Holly Endersby

Under a brilliant blue sky a brisk wind ruffles the native-grass pastures, and time seems to stand still as men walk toward the Pitchfork Land & Cattle Company cookhouse. Cowboys with sunburned, weather-worn faces and spurs jingling on boots enter a low white building, hang hats on hooks and find a place at the 25-foot-long table. A lot of good-natured kidding goes on, and laughter spices the hearty meal. For far more than a hundred years, this same scene has played out on the Pitchfork, near Guthrie in central West Texas.

Cattle have been the mainstay of the "Forks," as the ranch is known. A savvy combination of excellent ranch managers, a board of directors dedicated to taking care of their employees and

The signature gray color tells the tale—these are Pitchfork broodmares and foals.

189

the loyalty of the fine men and women who work on the ranch underwrite the Pitchfork's success. Today, with a unique combination of modernity and tradition, the ranch is renowned for producing both superb cattle and outstanding horses.

"Two words that define the Pitchfork are 'tradition' and 'consistency,'" horse manager James Gholson stated emphatically. James, who was wagon boss for 16 years before switching to his present position, said the traditional cowboy way is honored here on the Forks.

"I grew up wanting to be a Pitchfork cowboy," he shared. "My grandfather and uncle were both cowboys on the Forks, and I spent summers at the ranch as a kid."

James also said Pitchfork cowboys are hired to do only one thing—ride horses to check cattle.

"There's no multitasking required here," he explained. "The cowboys don't build fence, they don't farm and they don't put up hay. They stay horseback and work cattle. It's the way of life that the ranch represents that keeps people wanting to work here."

James Gholson served as the Forks' wagon boss for 16 years before becoming the ranch's horse manager.

A Solid Partnership

Cattleman Dan B. Gardner along with several other partners, including his friend and major financier, St. Louis businessman Eugene F. Williams, established the business on Dec. 13, 1883. The ranch consisted of 52,500 acres of open range and 9,750 native cattle purchased from Jerry Savage, who used the Pitchfork brand.

Because most of the partners knew little about the cattle business, Gardner became the ranch's first general manager, a position he held until shortly before his death in 1928. Unlike many ranches, the Pitchfork always has functioned as a corporation, with multiple investors and a strong board of directors. This all has proved a winning combination in developing one of the most famous and successful ranches in the West.

With Williams' death in early 1900, Gardner's steady leadership was even more critical. Under his management, the ranch increased in size to 97,000 acres, began to replace the native Longhorn cattle with Hereford cows and constructed windmill-driven wells to expand grazing options. In addition, the Pitchfork was fenced and cross-fenced into large 16,000- to 20,000-acre pastures. As the open-range days came to an end, enclosing the pastures made checking on 12,000 head of cattle easier and proved more efficient for gathering and branding.

Today, with the home ranch covering 165,000 acres, the Pitchfork is the only West Texas ranch that is larger now than when it started. Through boom and bust cattle prices, droughts and wartime shortages, the Pitchfork has endured where so many others have failed.

The Early Years

Gardner, although well-liked, expected the Pitchfork cowboys to work hard. Days off, except for Christmas and the Fourth of July, were nonexistent, and men were expected to work six days a week, and sometimes seven. Because all cows were pasture-bred, branding season lasted from six to seven months, something unthinkable today.

For their efforts, cowboys received between $25 and $30 dollars a month, and the wagon boss was paid $75. Wages were paid quarterly, with a running debit account for any clothes or supplies cowboys charged to the ranch. At the time, a good suit sold for $20, long underwear cost $5 and a hat was $3. Charged items automatically were deducted from a man's wages.

Bob Moorhouse managed the Forks from 1986 until mid-2007 and left his mark on both the horse and cattle programs.

The tools of the cowboy trade are thrown atop a fence, within easy reach for saddling the next horse to ride.

Food and housing were provided, but the living quarters were primitive at first. Wood for buildings is scarce in this brush-covered country. The early cowboys, as well as Gardner, lived in dugouts built into the bank along the South Wichita River. Not until 1898 were there conventional wooden structures built on the ranch.

After Gardner's death, the Pitchfork board of directors hired Virgil Parr as general manager. Parr was a widely respected agricultural economist with a background in animal husbandry from Texas A & M and Baylor University. He had managed a commercial farm and livestock business, and had worked as a U.S. Department of Agriculture agent before accepting the Pitchfork position.

On his arrival, Parr, a native Texan, began making changes. He quickly graded the herd bulls and kept only 90 of the 342 the ranch owned. By using better bulls, Parr hoped to breed better cattle. In 1935, Parr bought 100 purebred Hereford cows, as well as the outstanding Hereford bull Ike Domino. This formed the nucleus of the Pitchfork's purebred herd, which the ranch maintained for many years.

Breeding Better Horses

In addition to upgrading the cattle herd, Parr wanted to improve the ranch's horse operation.

Each cowboy has between seven and 10 horses on his string and takes full responsibility for the horses he uses for ranch work and competitive events.

Directors on the board, especially Eugene F. Williams' sons, agreed. The brothers, Eugene and Gates, purchased a Thoroughbred stallion named My Buddy, by Gold Enamel, to cross on the small native mares. In addition, a government remount program Thoroughbred stallion, Trimmer, was purchased in 1934. The sires added speed to their offspring, but did not produce the type of sturdy horse needed for extensive cow work.

Another manager, Rudolph Swenson, addressed that problem several years later and brought the first Quarter Horse stallion, Seal Brown, to the ranch in 1941. This sire, Seal Brown, produced a solid group of broodmares for the ranch. Swenson died in an accident before he had much time to put his stamp on the Pitchfork, but his resolve to improve the horse herd has carried on to this day.

The next manager, Douglas "D" Burns, held that position from 1942 until 1965. He continued to upgrade the horse herd by acquiring Joe Bailey's King from the neighboring Four Sixes Ranch. The young gray Quarter Horse stallion consistently stamped his offspring light gray with black manes and tails, coloration that soon became synonymous with Pitchfork horses.

Superior Cattle

D Burns, the fourth ranch manager, was well-liked but as hard-driving a man as his

With gloves, jacket and rope, and hat socked down against the Texas wind, Jacques Hughes is ready to start his day's work.

In the mid-20th century, herd sire Joe Bailey's King first stamped foals with the gray and black coloration that came to be associated with the Pitchfork horses.

193

predecessor Dan Gardner. Under D's leadership vacations once again were nonexistent, and men worked six and often seven days a week. But D worked just as tirelessly as the men he hired, a trait that is a hallmark of Pitchfork managers.

Although instrumental in upgrading the horse herd with his purchase of Joe Bailey's King, D's main focus was improving the Pitchfork's cattle. To do so, he culled many ranch bulls, replacing them with younger animals, as well as purchasing several prize-winning Hereford sires from the Midwest. His efforts paid off. By the mid-1940s, the ranch was recognized for the high-quality feeder cattle it raised.

That tradition of raising superior beef cattle remains with the ranch to this day although most of the animals sold now are black baldies. They are from Herefords, Black Angus and black baldy cows, with 95 percent Black Angus bulls being used.

When D retired in 1965 at age 70, he left the ranch in excellent condition. Most fencing had been replaced, equipment had been modernized and the cow and horse herds were recognized as among the best in the country.

Following D's retirement, Jim Humphreys became manager of the Forks. Under his able leadership, modernization continued at the ranch. Cowboys began using pickup trucks and trailers to haul horses around the ranch, and a helicopter was used when gathering cattle.

In 1970, the chuck wagon was retired, as the use of trucks and trailers made staying out on the range for days or weeks at a time a thing of the past. But the cowboys still rope and drag calves to the fire for branding. Sometimes the old ways are best.

In 1980, Jim had named Bob Moorhouse assistant manager. Bob had worked at the Forks following his graduation from Texas Tech in 1973, and with Jim's retirement in 1986, Bob became the Pitchfork Land & Cattle Company manager, a position he held until 2007.

A native Texan from a well-known ranching family, Bob proved an adept cattleman and worked to successfully market the ranch's horses and their athletic versatility. His years on the Forks also allowed Bob, an accomplished photographer, an excellent opportunity to chronicle ranch life from the late 20th century into the 21st.

David Ross provides the herd with a bit of guidance as the cattle are brought to the pens.

Cowboys on the Forks have only one job—ride horseback to check cattle.

Raising superior beef cattle has long been the goal at the Pitchfork Ranch.

Clay Timmons rides herd on Pitchfork cattle.

The Pitchfork Stallions

The Pitchfork's efforts to produce better cow horses have continued for decades, and in 1998 the ranch received the Best Remuda Award from the American Quarter Horse Association in conjunction with Bayer Animal Health and the National Cattlemen's Beef Association. Today Pitchfork horses are in high demand for both ranch work and competition.

"We have about 150 horses on the ranch today, with two-thirds of them being geldings used for daily work," said James Gholson. "Our horses continue to be popular at sales because the ranch has stayed up-to-date, using modern studs that cross well with the old pedigrees our mares carry."

Such names as Playgun, High Brow Cat, Grays Starlight and Dash for Cash are liberally sprinkled among today's ranch horses. Currently, the Pitchfork stands four stallions. Special Gun, a gray son of the famous Playgun, is used for breeding, as well as for showing in cutting and ranch-horse competitions.

"I started this horse, and he's one of my favorites," James admitted. "He's a pleasure to be around, and his colts show the same temperament. He can be in a pasture breeding the mares, and you can go up, catch him, haul him to a show and return him the next day. He's that good-minded. He was the 2005 RCHA—Ranch Cutting Horse Association—year-end champion, so he has lots of talent."

James said that Special Gun's winning show record is a testament to his ability, then added, "He's a tremendous herd sire for the ranch. We expect great things of his progeny in the future."

Another young stallion, Tejons New Star, by Grays Starlight and out of a Doc O'Lena-bred mare, also is used on ranch mares. Tejons New Star is just one example of the modern bloodlines the ranch judiciously uses on some of the mares.

Pay Forty Four, a 19-year-old son of Preferred Pay and a Chunky Monkey mare, has had a profound impact on the ranch herd.

"Pay Forty Four has been a tremendous asset to our breeding program," James affirmed. "Most of the geldings we sell are his, and his daughters in the mare band cross really well with our new studs."

James rode and showed Pay Forty Four as a 3-year-old and uses him for ranch work. "He has speed, size and athleticism. But what makes him so special is that he's so good-minded. You can rope or cut on him. He's the ideal ranch horse."

Pay Forty Four's offspring consistently have been high-sellers at ranch-horse sales. In 2007, for example, a gelding by Pay Forty Four sold for $44,000. The ranch sells approximately 10 geldings a year, and its horses are always in demand.

"It makes you feel good to produce a superior product that other people want," James said.

The ranch stands one stallion to outside mares, Cat Silver, a 1997 dappled gray stallion by High Brow Cat, the No. 1 cutting horse sire. Cat Silver is a National Cutting Horse Association money-earner, 2001 NCHA

Cowboys on the Forks still rope and drag calves to the fire for branding.

Windmill-driven wells have been used to expand the ranch's grazing options since the early 1900s.

Non-Pro Derby semifinalist and has earned an NCHA Certificate of Ability. The stallion also has earned 18.5 AQHA points and a Register of Merit in cutting.

Because Cat Silver's bloodlines are much in demand, he stands at the neighboring Four Sixes Ranch for breeding to outside mares. In addition, Cat Silver breeds 30 Pitchfork Ranch mares, and many of his daughters bred to Pay Forty Four produce solidly built horses for ranch work or competition.

At 14.3 hands and 1,200 pounds, Cat Silver, when crossed with the ranch mares, throws large colts. When crossed on smaller mares, he produces handy cutting or reining horses.

"Cat Silver is a pleasure to ride," stated James, who started the stallion as a young

horse. "He's well-mannered and always a gentleman.

"We're showing him in AQHA ranch-horse versatility classes to emphasize his talent. He's an exceptionally fluid mover, who also throws a lot of color. And today, color and gentleness are big sellers."

The ranch also owns a share in the syndicated stallion Paddys Irish Whiskey, by Peppy San Badger out of Doc's Starlight. Paddys Irish Whiskey stands at the Four Sixes and is among the top money-earners in the National Reined Cow Horse Association competition, as well as a leading sire in the National Reining Horse Association. When crossed on Pitchfork Ranch mares, often daughters of Pay Forty Four, Paddys Irish Whiskey sires excellent all-around horses.

The Pitchfork Ranch mares are counted on to contribute as much to their offspring as the stallions do. The consistently pretty mares are stout, with plenty of bone and muscle and, when crossed on the Forks modern sires, produce well-balanced foals with excellent conformation.

Remuda Sales

Pitchfork horses have been in high demand for many years, and the ranch typically hosts production sales every two years, which are social events as much as sales. Three other ranches participate in what is billed as the Return to the Remuda Sale.

"We bring out the chuck wagon and basically have a good old-fashioned party," James explained. "Folks like to come out, see the ranch, check out the horses and have a good time."

Pitchfork horses are sold at only one other ranch sale—the Best of the Remuda Sale, held in conjunction with other outfits that have received the AQHA's Best Remuda Award. No Pitchfork horses are sold through private treaty.

"We have no reserves at the two sales," James stated emphatically. "When we say a horse is for sale, it's for sale."

Versatile Pitchfork Horses

Bob Moorhouse said that growing interest in ranch rodeos and ranch-horse versatility competition has increased demand for the Forks' horses. That's because ranch cowboys also have begun to show the ranch's horses in recent years.

"Before we showed our horses, only a few people knew what great stock we had," Bob said. "Now Ranch Horse Association of America and the Ranch Horse Cutting Association events, and the AQHA ranch horse versatility classes have allowed us to introduce our horses to a much wider audience."

The exposure, he added has been great for the Forks. Such event competition is tough, which encourages continual skill-building among the cowboys. The ranch pays expenses for any show a cowboy enters with a ranch horse, and the rider keeps any purse he wins.

"A better cowboy makes a better horse," he stated. "And when a horse is sold, the cowboy who trained it gets a 10 percent commission, so they really have motivation for making good horses."

Each cowboy has between seven and 10 horses to ride and work on the ranch, but can show his horses, too. As they have in the past, today's cowboys choose horses on the basis of seniority. Each man starts his own horses and takes total responsibility for his string,

knowing he is expected to make them better horses for having been with him.

Bob acknowledged that ranch colts are started far differently than they were in the past. "Today we take it easy starting colts, helping them along, not forcing or frightening them. And I encouraged the men to use the training tapes we had on hand, as well.

This horse is a fine example of one worthy of the Pitchfork brand.

It's barely daylight when the remuda is gathered and cowboys prepare for the day's work.

"The men do a great job with the horses," he continued. "We used our horses and knew that they can perform. That pushed up the value of a ranch-raised horse, which allowed us to put more money into the studs."

The ranch wants to raise horses that can do it all, he explained. "The horses have to be fast to catch a cow, stop, turn and roll back to head them [the cattle] off and have good conformation to stay sound. This morning, the horse I was on had to jump a three-foot, barbed-wire fence at the last moment, and I knew he could do it. That's the same horse that I show in ranch horse competition.

"But horses are secondary to the main business, which is cattle," he stated emphatically.

The Ranch Report Card

The morning he was interviewed for this book, Bob and his crew had weighed and loaded 1,500 yearlings. This sale had special meaning for Bob; it was to be his last as Pitchfork manager, with his retirement coming only weeks later.

"We just made our biggest sale to date," Bob said. "We've focused on value-added with the Pitchfork beef. They are marketed as all-natural, age-verified animals, which is what the public wants."

Every animal has an electronically readable identification tag, which is crucial in today's international market, Bob explained. "Because we can track and age-verify cattle, they can be sold in Europe. With the concern about mad cow disease, this tracking is essential."

The biggest change in the ranch's cattle operation is in calving. The calving season used to run from spring through summer, but today it is a much shorter spring event. After weaning, the calves are turned out to fend for themselves, although supplemental feed is occasionally provided through the winter. The ranch has historically shipped yearlings, and continues that practice today.

Ten full-time cowboys ride herd, with seasonal help added when necessary. "All the calves are born in spring now," Bob confirmed, "and cowboys are expected to ride and care for the cows and nothing else. But I do appreciate a man who is willing to do anything asked of him."

Caring for cattle is serious business, according to the veteran ranch manager. "Getting a herd built up, getting the yearlings across the scales and hitting the market or hopefully above the market price has been my yearly report card."

Pitchfork Land & Cattle Company is a rarity—the only West Texas ranch larger now than when it was first established

The flags proudly fly at the Forks and have since 1883.

Pitchfork Land & Cattle Company Timeline

1883: Dan B. Gardner and partners, including Eugene F. Williams, established the ranch, which consisted of 52,500 acres of open range, and purchased 9,750 native cattle from Jerry Savage, who used the "Pitchfork" brand.

1900: St. Louis financier and Pitchfork partner Eugene Williams passed away.

1928: Dan Gardner passed away. The Pitchfork's first general manager until shortly before his death, Gardner increased the ranch to 97,000 acres, then cross-fenced the land to simplify checking the ranch's 12,000 head of cattle.

1930: Virgil Parr became general manager and began upgrading the herd bulls and cows, purchasing a group of purebred Hereford cattle.

1941: Rudolph Swenson, who became manager in 1940, brought the Quarter Horse stallion Seal Brown to the Forks.

1942: Following Swenson's unexpected death, Douglas "D" Burns became Pitchfork manager. During his tenure, which lasted until 1965, he acquired the stallion Joe Bailey's King from the Four Sixes Ranch.

1965: Jim Humphreys became manager of the Forks and moved Bob Moorhouse into the assistant manager's position in 1980.

1986: With Humphreys' retirement, Moorhouse became Pitchfork general manager. During his tenure, cowboys began training horses on their strings for ranch-horse and versatility competition, and cattle could be tracked and age-verified, thanks to improved technology.

1998: The Pitchfork received the Best Remuda Award from the American Quarter Horse Association, Bayer Animal Health and the National Cattlemen's Beef Association.

2007: Ron Lane, a Texas Tech graduate who was raised on the Four Sixes, became ranch manager. At 165,000 acres, the Pitchfork home ranch is the only West Texas ranch larger now than it was when first established.

He added that solid leadership from the Pitchfork's board of directors has helped the ranch stay profitable through the vagaries of Texas weather, the ups and downs of cattle markets and changing trends.

"The board members are very professional," he stated. "They understand it takes a lot of common sense, along with plenty of experience, to run a ranch successfully. The ranch employees work hard and, in return, the board takes care of the employees and really cares about them. They're good people who have kept the ranch's nose clean for 150 years. And the Pitchfork intends to keep that reputation going forward."

Ron Lane, a Texan raised on the Four Sixes Ranch, has been named Bob's successor—only the seventh manager of the historic outfit. His mission statement is inscribed on a small plaque in the old ranch office:

"Some things are made to last. At the Pitchfork Ranch, we hope the cowboy way of life will always be one of them. The people, and the spirit they lend to their work, make up the fabric of life in west Texas."

"We all know our jobs
and what's expected of us.
If something doesn't work out
right, it's our own fault.
We can ride the best horses
in the country, and it doesn't
cost us a penny."
Mack Daniel

12

W. T. WAGGONER ESTATE

By Holly Endersby

There's nothing shy about a Texas sunrise. It swaggers across the horizon in luscious strokes of red, mauve and orange. At daybreak, with gnarled black mesquite showing in silhouette against the skyline, the immensity of this country, and the huge ranches that dominate it, are stunning. For generations the Waggoner Ranch in north-central Texas has preserved this uniquely Western landscape and lifestyle. The Waggoner Ranch is the largest Texas ranch within one fence, using 12 line camps to manage 520,000 acres, almost 812 square miles. Cattle started the ranch, oil helped it grow, and horses always have been at the heart of the operation.

Although the Waggoner Ranch started with cattle and oil later proved a valuable asset, horses always have played the major roles.

Wes O'Neal, the ranch's former horse manager, has been with the Waggoner full-time since 1958.

Building a Dream

The lure of free land brought the Waggoner family of Tennessee to the Republic of Texas in the 1840s, where they first settled in what is now Hopkins County in northeast Texas. As with many a child then, young Dan Waggoner was destined to grow up quickly. His father died in 1848, and Dan took care of his mother and seven siblings. In 1849 he married 16-year-old Nancy Moore, but Dan's young wife died a mere year after their son, William Tom, called W.T. and also Tom, was born in 1852. After his wife's death, Dan left W.T. with his mother and sisters, and rode west looking for more land.

At that time, thousands of acres of free land were available for settlement in the Republic of Texas, and Dan quickly filed on 160 acres on Denton Creek near the present town of Decatur in Wise County. He moved there in the early 1850s with his mother, siblings, son, 240 Longhorns, six horses and one male slave. From that point, Dan began to seriously accumulate land.

In 1859, he remarried and 7-year-old W.T. came to live with his father and stepmother, Cecily Halsell Waggoner. These were hard times for the infant Texas cattle industry. The Civil War soon disrupted rail transportation, and the only beef buyer was the Confederate Army, paying just $10 a head. The low price, coupled with continuous Indian and outlaw raids, forced many cattlemen to sell out.

Dan Waggoner, however, held on. Once the war ended, rail lines pushed into Kansas, and the days of the famous Texas cattle drives began. Finally cattle ranchers began making serious money as more people left their rural roots for industrial jobs in cities. Beef was in high demand.

Establishing a Dynasty

Following his father's footsteps, W.T. early on was committed to becoming a cattle baron. At age 14, his stated ambition was "to run the best cattle outfit, own the best horses and do the most work of any man in the country." That vigor and determination became hallmarks of both father and son throughout their lives.

When W.T. turned 17, Dan made him a full partner in the ranch. At 18, W.T. helped drive a herd of cattle along the Chisholm Trail to Kansas, returning home with $55,000 in his saddlebags, an almost unimaginable amount in those days. At the ranch, Dan and W.T. shrewdly bought cattle at $8 a head for wintering. The following spring, W.T. drove their herd north to market, selling the cattle for $30 a head. From then on, the Waggoner empire grew rapidly, and by 1883 Dan Waggoner had investments not only in land and cattle, but also in five banks, three cottonseed-oil mills and a coal company.

Although he initially used cattle and horse brands consisting of a single "D" with numerals, W.T. ultimately began using three reversed Ds for his brand because rustlers could easily alter a single D. In recent years a number brand on a foal's left shoulder designates the dam and has a D underneath. The left hip number brand designates the year, and a sire brand is on the left thigh. As a result, ranch hands can easily determine a horse's age and breeding.

In 1877, W.T. wed Ella Halsell, his step-mother's 18-year-old sister. They were married in the county courthouse, and the bride's "attendants" were 12 of W.T.'s cowboy friends. The couple eventually would have five children, three of whom survived to adulthood—Electra, Guy and E. Paul Waggoner.

In 1885, W.T. and another Texas rancher negotiated a lease on thousands of acres of prime grazing land in Oklahoma Indian Territory. Situated across the Red River from Texas, the Oklahoma range became known as the "Big Pasture," and Quanah Parker, the great Comanche chief, approved the lease. W.T. and Quanah were alike in many ways, and their lives intersected often in the decades that followed, which resulted in a strong friendship growing between the men.

In 1903, Dan Waggoner died and left W.T. a vast cattle empire. But times were changing; free grazing and Indian lands were soon to be things of the past. With new settlers in the region, W.T. realized that he needed more deeded land and in a few short years bought thousands of additional acres. In 1905, the government revoked Comanche ownership and opened their lands for settlement. That fall, the Waggoners drove their cattle from the Big Pasture for the last time. The days of open range were gone.

But a 1902 event was to have a lasting impact on the Waggoner Ranch. While drilling for water, W.T. hit oil instead. Disgusted, he continued drilling for water. Oil was a nuisance, and any good cattleman knew the value of water. But by the 1920s and with the advent of the automobile, W.T.'s attitude about oil had changed, and the family got into petroleum development in a big way.

W.T.'s friend, the late great humorist Will Rogers, once said of the Waggoner Ranch, "I see there's an oil well for every cow."

Today, 160,000 acres have proven oil reserves. The short black wells still methodically pump oil as cattle graze contentedly on the surrounding lush grass.

Heirs to the Kingdom

In the early 1900s the Waggoner children married. Electra married A. B. Wharton. At one point, fearing that Electra would move East with her husband, W.T. built a lavish three-story Fort Worth mansion for the young couple. Today, a descendent, Albert B.

Trace Cribbs, who put himself through college by raising top horses, became the ranch's horse manager in 2001.

Wharton III, is co-director of the Waggoner Estate and lives with his wife, Jolene, at the ranch's Sachueista Headquarters. Appropriately, "sachueista" is an Indian term meaning "good grass."

Guy served as chairman of the Texas Racing Commission for a brief time in the 1930s when parimutuel betting was legal in the state. In 1939, following a move to New Mexico, where horse racing remained legal and where he established a ranch, Guy became chairman of the New Mexico Racing Commission.

W.T. and Ella had only one child who made the ranch his home as an adult—E. Paul. He loved Quarter Horses, rode each year in the Santa Rosa Roundup Parade and frequently opened the rodeo, an event he financed, astride his famous palomino, Goldie. His wife, Helen, was a gentle woman, who turned the grounds surrounding the ranch houses into lovely gardens. She took special care to plant roses, which her mother-in-law, Ella, loved so well. Today, these lush gardens still grace the ranch, adding green serenity to an otherwise arid landscape.

E. Paul's daughter, Electra Waggoner Biggs, was a talented sculptress who worked in bronze, She was well known for *Into the Sunset*, her larger-than-lifesize bronze of Will Rogers and his horse, Soapsuds, in Fort Worth, as well as for her busts of many important people of the day. The Waggoners' granddaughter, Helen Biggs Willingham, lives today with her husband, Gene, at the beautiful

Nowadays a broodmare prospect is halter-broke and ridden before joining the herd to raise foals for ranch use.

Each cowboy is expected to be a capable horse hand and has from seven to 10 head on his string to train and use.

Santa Rosa ranch site. Gene Willingham is a co-director of the estate.

Although a naturally frugal man, W.T. Waggoner was not afraid to pay for what he wanted. A devoted racing fan, he built the Arlington Downs Racetrack for $2 million in the early 1930s, in hopes the Texas state legislature would legalize parimutual betting; it did, although that law later would be repealed. From his 20-story Fort Worth office building, W.T. was, by all accounts, an easy touch for many civic causes. He would be proud to know that his descendents have remained staunch community supporters.

"The owners are simply great people," stated Trace Cribbs, horse manager for the ranch. "They are actively involved in many aspects of community service and are especially helpful in providing scholarships for local students."

W.T. died in 1934 and his wife, Ella, in 1959. But long before then, in 1923, they had placed the Waggoner Ranch in a family estate, where it remains today. An elegant marble office building in downtown Vernon, Texas, about 13 miles from the ranch headquarters, houses the estate offices.

Always About the Horses

Although the Waggoner fortune began with cattle and was greatly increased through oil revenue, the family always has loved good horses. Knowing that great cow horses made ranching on the vast outfit easier, W.T. always was on the lookout for likely stallions to cross on his sturdy ranch mares.

And, it was said, he always looked for a horse faster than his neighbor's. At one time, W.T. tried to buy the racing phenomenon Man O' War for $1 million. The stallion's owner, Colonel Bradley, sent back the check. W.T. then sent a blank check, asking Bradley to fill in the amount.

The Colonel's response: "Whenever the price can be set for the Eiffel Tower, a price will be set on Man O' War."

This might have been the only time Waggoner's money could not buy the horse he wanted.

The first famous Waggoner stallion was Yellow Jacket, a horse purchased at age 6 in 1916. Yellow Jacket was the result of line-breeding, with both his maternal and paternal grandsires being Lock's Rondo. This line, which got racing speed from Steel Dust and Shiloh blood via Old Billy, was particularly

Poco Bueno, the "Champion and Sire of Champions," was buried upright and his ranch grave marked with a 4-ton headstone.

attractive to W.T., who loved fast horses. W.T. used Yellow Jacket on select mares of the Steel Dust type to produce superior ranch cow horses. Breedings from Yellow Jacket produced two of the most influential Quarter Horse lines through the two stallions King and Skipper W.

Eventually W.T. gave Yellow Jacket to his friend, Texan Lee Bivins of Amarillo. Bivens bred the old stallion to three Peter McCue mares, who produced three outstanding stallions, one of which was Blackburn (P2228). Waggoner bought Blackburn and crossed the stallion on mares by ranch stallions Poco Bueno, Pretty Boy and Pretty Buck to produce many champions through the years.

Poco Bueno

But it was the horse W.T.'s son, E. Paul, bought as a yearling that changed much of Quarter Horse history—Poco Bueno. In 1945, E. Paul bought Poco Bueno as an untried 2-year-old colt for $5,700, a significant sum in those days. But the colt's breeding was impeccable, and E. Paul's impression of the young stallion would prove to be correct many times over. On the top side Poco Bueno was by King P-234, by Zantanon, often called the Mexican Man O' War for his racing prowess, by Little Joe, by Traveler. Poco Bueno's dam was Miss Taylor, by Old Poco Bueno, by Little Joe, by Traveler.

"Pokie" eventually grew to 14.3 hands, weighed 1,150 pounds and went on to win virtually every show he entered. Although he began his show career as a halter champion, his trainer, Waggoner Ranch foreman Bob Burton, thought the horse was naturally interested in cows so, as a 4-year-old, the stallion was switched to cutting.

Shortly thereafter, the new foreman, Lewis "Pine" Johnson, took over as trainer. Poco Bueno's wins from that point are legendary, and he stamped his offspring with the same great athleticism. Because the American Quarter Horse Association did not start keeping points until 1951, Poco Bueno returned to competition as a 7-year-old to accumulate his official AQHA Championship.

E. Paul insisted Poco Bueno be treated like a horse, despite his arena championships and his worth as a stallion. So each spring, Pokie was turned out to pasture-breed a band of mares. In all, he sired 405 registered foals in 24 foal crops. His get included 36 AQHA Champions, 163 halter-point earners and 118 performance-point earners, and his get also attained 84 Registers of Merit, 21 Superiors in halter and 13 Superiors in performance.

"Poco Bueno was a real nice, docile stallion," remembered Wes O'Neal, former ranch horse manager. "He was turned out every day, but toward the end of his life, he got arthritic and then foundered badly. Rather than have him suffer, he was put down."

Poco Bueno is buried in a standing position across from the ranch entrance on Texas Highway 283. A 4-ton granite headstone marks his grave, and the inscription reads: "Champion and Sire of Champions." In 1990, Poco Bueno was inducted into the AQHA Hall of Fame.

Horse Headquarters

The tidy barn, corrals, paddocks and hot-walkers identify Whiteface Line Camp near Electra, Texas, as headquarters for the ranch's horse program. The working cowboy's barn is

A look at a few of the 90-odd ranch-raised mares, and it's obvious why no new ones have been purchased "in eons."

nothing fancy, but has a place for all the necessary gear. Through the decades, hundreds of men and thousands of horses have passed through the barn's big double doors, including such men as Tony Hazlewood, Kenneth Handley and A.B. Wilkinson, who each worked 50 years on the ranch. Paul Whitley, who lived alone at a remote line camp and whose "country" consisted of 35,000 acres, was a Waggoner Ranch cowboy for 40 years.

Wes O'Neal, who still works horses for the ranch every day, also acts as an advisor to Trace Cribbs, the current Waggoner Ranch horse manager. Both are easy-going and soft-spoken, the type of men who make horses feel comfortable and who, just by their presence, are able to quieten a herd of nervous cows. Wes has been at the ranch full time since 1958, and Trace arrived in the early 1990s, but not as the horse manager.

"I have a computer-science degree and came here originally to convert the business from a mainframe computer to PCs," Trace explained. "But I've always been around horses and started getting involved here by picking some new stallions for the ranch."

Trace, who shuns the limelight, became manager of the horse operation in 2001.

Raised on a ranch in Altus, Okla., Trace has long had an eye for top horses.

"I started breeding horses when I was in 7th grade," he explained. "One of the colts I bred paid my way through college."

Wes' Recollections

Trace has great respect for Wes and is quick to credit him for offering sound advice and for saving a great broodmare band.

"Both our lives are better for working together," Trace said. "I would have been completely stupid to not keep Wes on with all he knows."

Wes, the quintessential lean, quiet cowboy, said cattle and horses drew him to the ranch originally. "I came because the ranch had lots of horses and cattle. All the work was done on horseback. We were paid $198.50 a month back then," he chuckled, "but we got free food and housing, too."

Wes recalls there were a lot of maverick cattle in those days. To gather them, the ranch maintained a remuda of 250 geldings and kept a chuck wagon out year-round. After working a number of positions on the ranch, Wes ran the horse-breeding operation for 25 years.

Approximately 11,500 mother cows provide ample work to keep the Waggoner Ranch cowboys busy.

"When I first got here, there wasn't a halter-broke mare on the place," Wes recalled. "They were all pasture-bred and really had not been handled."

Through time, he culled the broodmare band, keeping mares on the basis of solid conformation, disposition and bloodlines. Committed to the Quarter Horse breed, the ranch registered and put a brand on all its colts for the first time in 1957. The first time all the horses were gathered was in the early 1970s.

"We had close to 800 horses," Wes remembered. "Nobody knew until then how many there were."

The Broodmare Band Today

Today, the ranch has more than 400 horses. Due to a program Trace initiated, mares are caught in large lots, rather than being driven into chutes. Now, all mares are halter-broken and are ridden, as well, to help the men decide which ones to keep and which to sell.

The ranch uses its own stallions for artificially inseminating ranch mares, as well as shipped semen from syndicated stallions. The Waggoner Ranch also ships semen for outside mares. With precision accuracy, the ranch boasts an excellent 98 percent conception rate. Trace also has been using embryo transfers successfully to broaden the ranch bloodlines.

A total of 90 broodmares call the Waggoner Ranch home. Wes explained that the ranch's mare pedigrees are still heavy with King bloodlines. "In the early days, we often traded or borrowed studs from the King Ranch. A lot of times we traded mares with them, as well."

Because the ranch focuses on producing 15-hand geldings from cutting-horse bloodlines, a lot of the ranch mares and their foals look similar. To chart a mare's offspring, colts are branded in three places to denote the dam and sire, as well as a single D referencing the ranch brand.

"The mares have been with us a long time, and we know what kind of colt each makes. We're in the business of producing ranch horses that can also do well in versatility competitions. There's a good market for that kind of horse," Trace said.

Ranch stallions are only as good as the broodmares they cover, and the ranch has an enviable band of truly great mares. At a 2004 Fort Worth Stock Show horse sale, the Waggoner Ranch had the high-selling horse.

Experience shows. Jimbo Glover casts a knowing eye on the Waggoner cow herd as a well-seasoned mount waits to do his rider's bidding.

The 3-year-old filly, Roosters Senorita, by Gallo del Ciello, nicknamed Rooster, sold for $33,000.

"We haven't bought mares for eons," Trace declared. "We still have what people need. Our horses are very functional and last forever. They have a lot of cow in them, along with short backs, good withers and solid bone structure."

Ranch Stallions Today

Early in his tenure at the ranch, Wes began upgrading the stallions. "We paid $15,000 for Peppys Pavo as a yearling in 1977, and everyone thought he would bankrupt the ranch," he recalled.

As did Wes, Trace continues to upgrade the ranch stallions. To complement the mares, he wants stallions approximately 15 hands, with good withers, dark feet, deep heart-girths, hocks that line up straight and good minds. With such criteria in mind, Trace has added several stallions to the ranch line-up, bringing today's championship bloodlines to the legendary Waggoner mare band.

Greyt Whiz, a fine 2003 stallion by Top Sail Whiz, whose dam and grand-dam were both National Reining Horse Association Futurity finalists, is being worked by reining trainer Doug Milholland. Doug, who has joined the Waggoner Ranch full-time after decades of managing his own show barn and racking up numerous championships through the years, enjoys being able to train for just one client.

Poco Tuck Zero, a classic-looking Poco Bueno grandson who has 97 percent foundation bloodlines, was sold, and then Trace brought him back to the ranch again in 2001 to continue the famous line. Poco Tuck Zero was sired by Poco King Tuck, and two young ranch stallions, Double My Whiskey and Justa Swinging Poco, are Poco King Tuck grandsons. Whiskey, whose dam is Miss Double Tuck, placed fifth in the 2007 NRHA Derby intermediate-open division.

According to Doug, Double My Whiskey has athletic ability in spades. "He's incredibly physical with a big stop and tons of turns," the trainer said.

Focusing on cutting and reining progeny that will also make good working ranch horses, Trace added Doc O Boots, by Grays Starlight and out of Doc'O Lenita, to the

The ranch focuses on producing cutting-bred, 15-hand geldings that can capably handle a day's work and perform well in ranch-versatility events.

Tradition reigns on the Waggoner Ranch as a cowboy drags a calf within reach of the ground crew.

The Waggoner branding crew typically operates smoothly and efficiently, thanks to the men's many years of experience.

This contemporary Waggoner Ranch cowboy seems little different from those hands in sepia-toned portraits made more than a century ago.

stallion roster. This stallion, Trace said, "will eat up a cow."

Milholland agreed, adding, "He's as intense on a cow as anything I have ever ridden."

These traits will continue to strengthen the huge reservoir of "cow" found in the Waggoner Ranch horses. Harkening back to Poco Bueno, and the superior athleticism and trainability of that prepotent sire, Trace really likes Justa Swinging Poco, the 2002, 15-hand sorrel stallion by Justa Swinging Peppy, by Peppy San Badger, and out of WT Poco Lady Heart, by Poco King Tuck and out of The Ladys Heart.

"We think Justa Swinging Poco may be a sleeper sire for us," Trace commented. "His colts are super-gentle and have a lot of bone. And his babies are real people horses. They come right up to you in the pasture."

The ranch now stands Smartest, a 2003 son of Smartest Chic O Lena, by Smart Chic O Lena, in addition to two young stallions by High Brow Cat, the No. 1 cutting-horse sire in 2007. The young horses, Cat Man Do and Purrfect Timing, are destined to show in National Cutting Horse Association events.

"The High Brow Cat babies are all really trainable and excellent movers," Trace explained, "and a finished horse by him sells very well."

Additionally, the ranch owns a share of the syndicated stallion, Paddys Irish Whiskey, an NRHA leading sire, whose offspring have won in reining, cutting, reined cow horse and roping events. His athletic ability crossed with the Waggoner mares should produce very versatile horses.

"I've never seen Wes so excited about colts," Trace added.

According to Trace, the ranch's two main trainers, Doug Milholland and Greg Ray, Wes O'Neal's son-in-law, make a great combination. "Doug's a fantastic trainer. He's shown reining horses for years and doesn't blow his

When a cowboy's spurs showcase the outfit, obviously he rides for the brand—three reversed Ds.

*With a
little bit of
assistance
from the
"old" hand,
the next
generation
is well on
its way to
earning
its ranch-
cowboy
credentials.*

horses apart. Doug will be great for these young show horses."

Greg, Trace added, is great working the 2-year-olds. "Greg is so good with the colts. He starts them just right. I've seen him have a colt saddled in 15 minutes."

The Cowboy Life

The Waggoner Ranch always has been progressive in its treatment of employees. Mack Daniel, who has been at the ranch 24 years and is boss of the headquarters crew, explained the working arrangements.

"The unmarried men live in a bunk-house and eat in the cookhouse," he said. "Married men get a house at one of the line camps. The ranch pays for utilities, gives us free beef, provides health insurance and a retirement plan."

Today, the ranch is split into 74 pastures, and men come home each evening. In the old days, Mack recalled, cowboys camped and ate from a chuck wagon for days at a time. However, the ranch still runs a dozen line camps to cover the far-flung property.

Men living at the line camps are anomalies in today's world. They relish the solitude and the responsibility of taking care of their areas of the ranch. Joe O'Neal has been on the Waggoner 44 years; Cotton Daniel, 32 years; Bobby Daniel, 30 years; and Rick Stone, 27 years.

The headquarters crew is equally long-employed, with wagon boss Jimbo Glover clocking 31 years. Weldon Hawley, the ranch's cattle manager, has been on the Waggoner for 22 years, and seven cowboys have logged from five to 11 years on the ranch, as well.

According to Weldon, the reason is simple: "It's dedication to ride for the brand."

Mack said the best part of working on the Waggoner Ranch is the ability to be your own boss most of the time. "We all know our jobs and what's expected of us," he explained. "If something doesn't work out right, it's our own fault. We can ride the best horses in the country, and it doesn't cost us a penny."

Obviously the Waggoner horses are a big draw for the cowboys. Each cowboy has seven to 10 horses to train and use, and all the cowboys are expected to be capable horse hands. Each May the cowboys select 2-year-old colts to add to their strings. The most senior man chooses his first, with the least senior hand selecting his last.

Even Waggoner oil wells carry the ranch brand.

Premium Beef

The 30 ranch cowboys need plenty of good horses. The cowboys oversee a herd of approximately 11,500 mother cows and 650 to 700 bulls.

Weldon Hawley said the focus is on premium beef. "All our yearlings are sold as natural beef, with no hormones or feed additives, other than all-natural minerals, used."

An active farm division of 26,000 acres produces wheat, oats, milo and hay for sale and for use as feed on the ranch. As a result, the ranch's self-contained nature partially insulates it from the vagaries of market feed prices, with which other, smaller ranches must contend.

Each year, Mack selects about 1,700 replacement heifers, which include Herefords, black baldies, Black Angus and some Red Angus. The remaining cattle are sold in huge lots at auctions or through private treaty. Each calf is weighed and measured so the ranch can track and evaluate the type of calves each bull sires.

"We know the product of each bull," Weldon stressed. "We cannot manage if we

The brand with three reversed Ds is recognized nationwide as a hallmark of quality horses.

can't measure our product. We record everything now, from pasture status reports to bull turnout spreadsheets. And our cowboys get regular printouts."

Mack and his men gentle replacement heifers by riding horseback around the heifers in large pens, by having the ranch kids feed the heifers and by teaching the heifers to come to the feed truck when a siren sounds. All these things make the cattle much easier to handle.

Still a Necessity

Despite modern conveniences, good horses are still necessary on the Waggoner Ranch. Weldon said the ranch counts on the horses having a lot of cow in them to work cattle. "They're good rope horses, too. We still drag calves to the fire for branding, so the horses we use work hard."

It usually takes five years to make a superior ranch horse, and by that time, the geldings often are offered at one of the ranch production sales.

"It's hard for a man to give up a horse he's worked so long," Weldon admitted. "But the

Sachueista, or Zacaweista, as the headquarters sometimes are known, is an Indian term for "good grass," which the ranch has in abundance.

W.T. Waggoner and wife Ella placed "the largest ranch under one fence in Texas" into the Waggoner Estate in 1923.

Waggoner Ranch Timeline

1848: Dan Waggoner's father, who had moved the family from Tennessee to Texas, died, leaving Dan responsible for his mother and siblings.

1852: William Tom Waggoner, known as W.T. and Tom, was born to Dan and wife Nancy Moore, who passed away a year later.

1869: W.T. became a full partner in his father's ranch.

1877: W.T. married Ella Halsell, and three of their children survived to adulthood—Electra, Guy and E. Paul Waggoner.

1885: W.T. and another Texas rancher negotiated an Oklahoma Indian Territory pasture lease with Comanche chief Quanah Parker.

1902: While drilling for water, W.T. hit oil, then the bane of a cattleman's existence.

1916: W.T. purchased the stallion Yellow Jacket.

1923: W.T. and wife Ella Waggoner placed "the largest ranch under one fence in Texas" into the Waggoner Estate.

1934: W.T. Waggoner died.

1945: E. Paul Waggoner purchased Poco Bueno, who was foaled in 1944, for $5,700, a high price for the times.

1957: The Waggoner outfit registered and branded all the ranch colts.

1960: Dan Waggoner became one of the original inductees into the Cowboy Hall of Fame at the National Cowboy and Western Heritage Museum.

1969: "Champion and Sire of Champions" Poco Bueno died and was buried upright just across from the Waggoner Ranch entrance.

1970s: The first complete Waggoner Ranch horse gather resulted in a tally of almost 800 head.

1990: Poco Bueno was inducted into the American Quarter Horse Hall of Fame.

1994: The Waggoner Ranch received the American Quarter Horse Association Best of the Remuda Award.

1998: The Waggoner Ranch received the American Cowboy Culture Award for Ranching.

1999: The Waggoner Ranch received the Charles Goodnight Award for contributions to the livestock industry.

cowboy gets a percentage of the sale price, so that incentive helps."

Through the years, the Waggoner Ranch has won many awards including the 1998 American Cowboy Culture Award for Ranching; the 1999 Charles Goodnight Award; top ranch honors in the Wichita Falls Ranch Round Up in 1988, 1989, 1990, 1993 and 2000; and the AQHA Best Remuda Award in 1994. Thanks to Poco Lena, Poco Mona, Poco Stampede and Snipper W, the ranch also is a leading breeder of NCHA Hall of Fame members, as well as among the top breeders of AQHA Champions.

The Best Accolades

But the best accolades come from ranch employees.

"We've always been treated like family on the Waggoner Ranch," Mack Daniel said.

Weldon Hawley added that there is a reason why, when compared with many ranches, the Waggoner has very little turnover. "It's because the owners are so good to work for. When employees are treated well, people tend to stay on. Unlike a lot of other ranches, the owners actually live here. That makes a big difference."

With an emphasis on quality in all the ranch undertakes, as well as its history of treating employees with respect for jobs well done, the Waggoner Ranch is destined to remain one of the greatest custodians of Texas' ranching culture.

Dan and W.T. would be proud.

13

GANG RANCH

By Tim O'Byrne

On the very fringe of North American civilization, with nothing but wild Canadian mountains to serve as the western boundary, the massive Gang Ranch beckons, seducing the challenger to try his luck at grazing cattle on central British Columbia's open arid plateaus and green alpine meadows. The deep Fraser River canyon, which marks the eastern boundary of the 770,000-acre cow outfit, is silent except for the slow hiss of turbulent olive-green water flowing toward the Pacific Ocean.

The river's east bank feels safe, connected somehow to the rest of the world. The forbidding expanse of land emanating

At its peak, the Gang Ranch controlled more than 4 million acres of deeded and Crown land, or Canadian federal grazing allotments.

Larry Ramstad, who became general manger in 1989, set the Gang Ranch on the road to recovery.

Kelly Cornforth is cowboss at the Gang, which runs cattle on some of the most remote, rough country in North America.

Far From Their Southern Home

Jerome, Ezekiel and Thaddeus Harper, raised in West Virginia's Blue Ridge Mountains, shared a sparse upbringing with 13 brothers and sisters. Understandably, when the time came for them to leave their parents' small Tucker County ranch, the three brothers headed west to spread their wings. They were free from the encumbrances of such a large family, who seemed tied fast to a handful of acres and hardship.

The year was 1848, and western expansion was in full swing. San Francisco was enjoying a boomtown atmosphere brought on by the California gold rush, and the sweet aroma of opportunity was the reason for the Harper brothers' timely arrival in 1849.

America was growing during the last half of the 19th century, and the western borders tended to shift like clouds in the sky. The Republic of California was still one year away from admission into the union as the 31st state. The Oregon Territory ran north to the border of the colony of British Columbia, an almost unbelievable 365,000 square miles of mountainous land north of the 49th parallel in present-day Canada. Belonging to the British Crown, the fledgling province encompassed a total landmass larger than the combined states of Washington, Oregon and California.

Until the northwestern United States' border was finally defined in the Treaty of Oregon in 1846, Britain and the United States simply shared the entire Pacific-western area, from the northern California border to the Yukon's wilds. There was ample of room for everybody.

Loose borders such as these played well into the hands of Jerome and Thaddeus as they planned their exodus northward in 1854. Ezekiel stayed in San Francisco. His brothers left the port city to follow the sweat-stained miners, whose dreams were to be realized or lost in the newfound British Columbia gold fields.

Two personality types answer a gold strike's tantalizing call—those who succumb to the "fever," and those who follow along at a reasonable distance to administer to the needs of the afflicted. The Harpers considered themselves the latter, and with great optimism they set up a sawmill when they arrived and, almost as fast as the documents could be printed, secured deeds to ranchland near the town of Kamloops. The brothers soon

from the western shore, however, is referred to by locals as the Chilcotin (chill-KOE-tuhn), a term derived from the sometimes volatile Chilcotin Indian band who made the area their ancestral home. The Chilcotin is a mysterious place, where an outsider might never truly feel at home. Black bear, cougar, deer and moose significantly outnumber humans in these mountains, and the cold winters can be long, dark and deathly quiet.

None of that mattered to the Harper brothers.

supplied fresh-cut lumber and juicy, grass-fed steaks to those toiling away their lives. Fresh beef was a commodity very much welcomed by the voracious appetites of miners up and down the golden corridor.

The Fraser's Wild Western Shore

As the Harper bothers worked their way north on the old Fraser River Trail in 1864, following the gold rush with a herd of fat cattle and acquiring property as they went, they came to Dog Creek, an area along the river's east bank. Many travelers before them had gazed with covetous eyes at the pristine grasslands swaying in the breeze on the Chilcotin side of the river. But none had made an attempt to set foot there; the river was too wide, too cold and much too treacherous.

Thaddeus, as the story goes, made visual contact with a band of native Chilcotins camped on the western shore. He somehow persuaded them to cross the river in their log canoe and ferry him back to discuss his proposal to set up a cattle outfit on their side of the river. His proposal succeeded.

No journal entry tells the details of how this unorthodox meeting progressed, but Thaddeus and the natives agreed to a handshake boundary, which allowed the white man to run cattle unimpeded while the natives continued living in their traditional manner. As the Harpers' land acquisitions continued to grow, the Pacific Northwest was gaining a reputation as a major beef supplier for railroad crews building the Canadian Pacific Railway's western portion.

The Big Drive

In 1870, Jerome was kicked by a horse and suffered severe head trauma. He never fully recovered, and left his brother in the north country, retiring to San Francisco's relative comfort. Jerome died there three years later, alone in the bathtub of his suite.

Jerome's death did not seem to slow down Thaddeus, who, in 1876, organized the longest trail drive of British Columbia cattle ever recorded. He and his local cowboy crew put together a herd of about 1,200 head and pointed them toward a distant market opportunity in Chicago, Ill.

The brazen plan was to drive the herd overland down existing trails all the way to Salt Lake City, and then ship the cattle by

The arid ranch gets just enough moisture annually to grow feed for wintering the cattle herd.

Cattle are moved periodically to satisfy the grazing program established by the forestry service and the ranch manager.

rail the rest of the way. The journey's first leg lasted several months and brought the cowboy crew as far as Walla Walla, Wash., where they wintered the herd on grasslands protected by the state's mild interior climate.

In spring 1877, with the herd and many cowboys far from home, it became apparent that Chicago was not an economically feasible destination. So the crew bent the herd southwest, heading for San Francisco. After 18 months on the trail, Thaddeus pocketed a backslapping profit of $70 per head.

Partners, Boom and Bust

In a strange coincidence 14 years later in 1884, Thaddeus, just as his brother, was thrown from his horse and kicked in the head. Drs. Davie and Helmcken, attending physicians in the city of Victoria, reported their patient had incurred broken teeth, a broken jaw and a fractured skull. The injuries, coupled with other health concerns, resulted in a long, slow recuperation period that gave Thaddeus much time to consider the future.

The next year he initiated an earnest search for a financial partner to assist in keeping the ranch solvent and growing. He found such support in an English publisher, Thomas Galpin, and together they created the single largest cattle ranch in Canada—the Western Canadian Ranching Company Ltd. Galpin and his business partners later took possession of the operation in 1891, leaving Thaddeus to retire.

Thaddeus had long suffered from a deadly medical condition. Secondary syphilis, likely contracted during visits to California brothels in his wild and frivolous youth, had taken its toll on his health. In 1891 he retired to Victoria, and in 1898, at age 65, Thaddeus Harper passed away. There was no record of his having wives, children or heirs of any kind. He left the Gang Ranch, formally known as the Western Canadian Ranching Company Ltd, and all its holdings to his English business partner, publisher Thomas Galpin.

In the following decades the ranch held its own, continuing to raise succulent, grass-fed beef. At its peak in the 1930s, the ranching operation was scattered from the shores of Kamloops Lake all the way to Riske Creek, covering more than 4 million acres of deeded and Crown, or Canadian federal government, grazing allotment.

But after World War II, the population's general mindset changed and mechanized agriculture led to the decline of the large work crews of men and horse teams that had kept the ranch functioning. In 1947, after several hard and lean years, the Western Canadian Ranching Company Ltd. was sold to American cattlemen Dr. William Patrick Studdert and Floyd Skelton.

The Gang Ranch Name

In the beginning, the Gang Ranch was not formally registered or recognized by its now famous name. The official ranch moniker, adopted legally when the ranch was established as a limited corporation around 1885, ended up as the anything-but-romantic Western Canadian Ranching Company Ltd. Prior to that, the outfit, one of the Harper brothers' collective holdings, was simply known as part of the Harper Ranch.

The Gang Ranch is basically a nickname, derived from the "gang," a piece of new technology that arrived on the North American agricultural scene in approximately 1870. This heavy steel plow, pulled by a team of horses, could be fitted with a "gang" of shovels, a series of ground-turning blades, instead of only a single plowshare. The story goes that,

at some point in history, a gang plow was brought to the ranch and put to use during the outfit's early years, but no record of a machine has been historically verified. The name, however, lives on.

Embracing the Challenges

The wide, well-groomed gravel road leaves the pavement 20 miles southwest of the logging town of Williams Lake, Canada. The roadbed must be structurally sound to support thousands of semi-loads of heavy logs trucked annually from the Chilcotin and headed for the sawmills in town. Driving a four-wheeled vehicle down the switchbacks into the Fraser River valley and up the other side can be an eye-opener for any flatlander. But maneuvering a loaded log truck, chained-up for traction in the dead of winter, is a serious test of skill and nerves.

Two bridges allow ranch access from civilization. The only one truly strong enough to support a semi-load of cattle or logs spans a steep, rocky gap over the Chilcotin River at the ranch's north end. In 2006, the supporting bridge timbers caught fire, and the entire structure collapsed into the Chilcotin's raging

A veritable sea of cattle grazes the 770,000-acre outfit.

waters below. That caused one of the most serious stumbling blocks with which the Gang Ranch has had to deal in recent memory.

"The collapse of that bridge basically shut down our competitive ability to ship calves in the fall," explained Larry Ramstad, the ranch's general manager since 1989. Ramstad, a veteran of commercial ranching in British Columbia, has spent his entire working life operating or managing such historic cow outfits as the Quilchena and Cotton Ranches.

Fortunately, his wife, Bev, was born and raised to the lifestyle. When Thaddeus Harper took that long cattle drive to San Francisco in 1876, Bev's great-grandfather, Johnny Twan, was there. He was one of 10 cowboys listed in the archives as having made that record-breaking trip.

The Gang Ranch was in need of a cow man such as Larry Ramstad. During the tumultuous years from 1950 until the late 1980s, a host of individuals who possessed little or no savvy of the complex steps involved in running an operation such as the Gang literally had accosted the ranch.

Current owner Ibrahim Afandi, a Saudi Arabian partner in BSA Investments Ltd., had the wisdom to realize that his role as the Gang Ranch's absentee owner, assumed in 1987, was a challenging one. His greatest challenge, however, was to find a capable individual possessing a work ethic above reproach, who would do whatever was necessary to manage the massive outfit's daily operations. Nothing else would suffice; there was simply too much at stake, and it would prove impossible for an outsider to fairly audit the complex management minutia that make up the Gang's big picture. In a move that received an approving nod from all major players in British Columbia's close-knit cattle community, Ramstad was put in charge.

During the region's short May-to-September growing season, most of the weather comes from the west—in the form of huge Pacific storm systems that spiral inland from the ocean some 250 miles distant. But by the time the storms have crossed the rugged mountain ranges, their moisture is depleted, leaving very little rain to fall on the arid interior east of the tall peaks. The Gang Ranch might see only 25 centimeters—less than 10 inches—of precipitation annually, half in the form of snow, the other half as rain. That is

Ranch horses here vie for top honors in an arena that has "quicksand at one end, thick timber at the other, and a thousand miles between."

229

barely enough to grow the 6,000 tons of feed needed annually to maintain the ranch cattle through the winter and spring months until the grass comes once again.

Nothing Taken for Granted

Water, electricity and communication with the outside world often are taken for granted throughout much of North America today. But none of these key elements of modern life came easy to Gang Ranch residents.

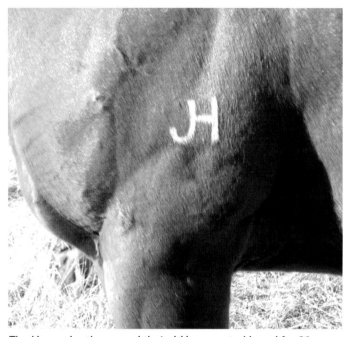

The Harper brothers used their J-H-connected brand for 20 years before British Columbia established a formal brand registration.

The ranch headquarters are at 2,150 feet above sea level. One of the first engineering challenges, in order to supplement the lack of irrigation and plumbing water there, involved building a small dam on remote Gaspard Lake, many miles to the west and much higher than the ranch site.

Water from the dam follows an extensive system of irrigation ditches and canals that snake the precious commodity into 1,500 hundred acres of meticulously groomed hay fields surrounding the headquarters. The summer months provide enough heat to grow two cuttings of alfalfa-and-grass mixed hay and, if the fall is mild, a third cover is nurtured along to provide late fall grazing for calves after the first freeze.

Electricity long has been considered a luxury on the Fraser River's western shore. Situated on a grassy bench between Gaspard and Churn Creeks, the Gang headquarters is among the most remote ranch settings in North America. Overhead power lines, the kind that traverse almost every rural American road, can cost up to $1,000 per pole to install. An average ranch lane in a typical cow-country setting might have 30 or more poles providing service, but outfits many miles off the blacktop require hundreds of poles to make the distance.

The sheer number of power poles required to service Gang Ranch buildings would be cost-prohibitive, especially given that the ranch is at the end of the power line, and the nearest

Approximately 80 head in the remuda serve the Gang Ranch cowboys, usually a crew of seven or so men.

The Chilcotin is scenic country, but can be dangerous to horse and rider, given the difficulty of locating them and getting medical attention to them.

A ranch-owned and –operated power plant provides electricity at the Gang, but only the cookhouse, main house, office and shop have telephones.

Durable cabins and catch pens occasionally interrupt miles of wide-open country on the British Columbia ranch.

neighbor is at least 20 hard and difficult miles eastward. Crossing the Fraser River with a power line would require massive steel towers on either side to safely facilitate the span.

The only other economical option—install a ranch-owned and -operated power plant. It consists of primary and backup diesel generators servicing a small system of private lines going to ranch houses, the main office, cookhouse, shop, barn and irrigation pumps. Sometime during the late 1950s, the ranch system was complete, and likely with much mock fanfare, the cook ceremoniously flicked on the cookhouse light for the very first time.

At the cookhouse, built in 1917, the big black bell still rings before every meal. It is a daily reminder to all within earshot that tradition means a great deal in this remote cattle country. As is common and traditional on large North American ranches, strict rules govern the cookhouse. Cowboys remove their boots before entering and refrain from using foul language. Each patron must take his dishes to the sink after each meal and, as he leaves, thanks the cook.

The first thing the Gang Ranch farm boss does every single morning, year-round, is shut down the generator to check the oil, fluids and belts. Then he fires up the big machine again, confident that it will last another day. If, by chance, the generator should fail overnight during the critical winter months, the farm boss, wakened by the eerie silence, instinctively sits bolt upright in bed and yells, "The generator's down!"

At this point he rushes into the dark, cold night and cranks the back-up generator until the primary machine can be diagnosed and fixed. Without power to heat water lines or buildings, the ranch would be frozen solid by breakfast time. These are the facts of life on the remote ranch, and people rapidly learn to adjust, to ensure their own survival.

Today's world relies heavily on high-tech communication. Imagine, however, living in a house that has no landline or cell-phone service. Gang Ranch telephones can be counted on the fingers of one hand. The office, shop, main house and cookhouse have lines, but employee housing situated on the headquarters' outskirts has none.

Cowboys in remote, pack-in cow camps use solar-powered satellite radiophones to communicate with ranch headquarters. Old-timers would be amazed at the benefits of this new technology. Sometimes, however, the

Most who live in isolated ranch houses tune in when a radio segment with messages for backcountry dwellers airs daily.

The initials in the Gang Ranch brand are those of Jerome Harper, who helped his brother, Thaddeus, establish the outfit.

ranch two-way radio reception is poor due to the rough terrain and mountains blocking the signal. When things get dicey, and someone needs to communicate anyway, one click on the radio-microphone means "no," and two clicks mean "yes."

Isolation and Predation

A daily AM radio segment, known to mountain residents simply as "Time for Messages," originates from a tiny Williams Lake studio. Every day at precisely 1 p.m., the announcer reads a list of messages to intent listeners located in isolated ranch houses and logging camps, or on Indian reservations.

Journals in ranch cabins and ranch-style graffiti on logs mark the onetime presence of those who have worked on and visited the Gang.

The jeans, boots and spurs might be a little worn, but they have met the challenges of life on the Gang.

Each message is a snapshot of the simple, yet colorful Chilcotin life.

"Good afternoon, everyone, this is WKLM Radio messages," the pleasant announcer says to all those who have tuned in to get a jump-start on the latest gossip. "Anita Jimmy, your niece will meet you Friday at the dentist's office. In today's lost and found, a small herd of cows was spotted heading down Canhim Lake Road, past the water treatment plant. If they're yours, please come and round them up."

Every ear in the Chilcotin waits until the very last message is read on the crackly radio before the people turn back to their daily lives.

The isolation of being 60 hardcore miles from the nearest town is considered a blessing by most ranch employees, who have chosen that lifestyle and leave only a few times each year to get their fill of civilization. Every Wednesday a white van, which locals still refer to as "the stage," travels the long, loop road running from the town of Clinton through the Fraser River valley's backcountry ranches. At noon the stage arrives at the Gang Ranch store and post office, amid a gathering of ranch residents waiting for mail, parts and/or supplies from town. Then the little white stage pulls out of the ranch yard with the promise of returning next week.

Establishing a cattle ranch in the wildest part of Western Canada comes with yet another price. Predation, mostly in the form of black bear attacks on calves, can certainly be considered a cost of doing business in the backcountry. But spikes in wolf and bear populations in recent years have been implicated in major increases in livestock-related predatory attacks.

Other wildlife exacts a toll on the ranch economy, too. At nightfall during the spring and fall, as many as 1,000 mule deer can be foraging on ranch hay meadows. Fenced test plots indicate that deer might be pre-harvesting up to 50 percent of the first crop of rich alfalfa-grass mix in select areas.

Risks to cattle grazing in the Chilcotin also include poisoning from water hemlock or blue-green algae, or an accidental collision with a heavily loaded logging truck on open range. Plus, cattle can bog down in mud while drinking water from natural springs. But deer, bears, wolves, springs and vegetation belong here, too. And, as with all ranches truly perched on the edge of a northern wilderness, the Gang Ranch has learned to coexist as best it can.

The Map Tells The Tale

Long before aerial photography, global-positioning systems and backcountry satellite imaging, there were forestry maps, some hand-drawn works of art dating from the 1940s and '50s, painstakingly colored and printed individually on linen. Such names as Hungry Valley, Lost Valley and Graveyard Valley inspire the most adventurous cowboys to pack bedrolls and grub for long rides into the high country.

Hungry Valley was named for the feeling cowboys get three weeks after their arrival in a backcountry camp, when food supplies start to run low. It often has been said that, at the beginning of the high-country cattle turnout, Gang Ranch cowboys were handed a box of .30.30-caliber shells and a sack of spuds, and told not to come back to headquarters unless they were near death.

Across the mountain range is Lost Valley, with an inviting cabin and horse corral, and even farther beyond is Graveyard Valley. The outfit's final, distant, pack-in cow camp is named for the Indian graves that lie easily within haunting distance of the tiny one-room log cabin.

The valley floors and upland sidehills are covered in forbs, sedges and mixed grasses that provide unequalled cattle nutrition during the short summer months. A huge drawback, however, is sharing the timbered mountainsides with swarms of blood-sucking mosquitoes, trillions of biting deer flies and healthy numbers of large, hungry, meat-eating predators, all just waiting to serve up a tasty mammal for dinner.

The breathtakingly beautiful and rugged Gang Ranch backcountry is sacred to those few and fortunate people who travel it horseback. Guest journals in the cabins date back decades, and each visitor, whether he worked for the ranch or passed through

As eye-catching as it is serviceable, this fence line seems to stretch for miles through the Canadian ranch country.

on a recreational pack trip, has left a heart-felt entry in ink, pencil or even charcoal. Vandalism is nonexistent; those with enough mettle to pack a horse and find their way here would never break a cabin window or leave without gathering wood for the next person. To do so would be to disrespect a primitive law of survival that protects visitors to these quiet mountains.

Ten Years Make A Herd

The ranch runs more than 3,000 head of cattle on 770,000 acres, but only 34,000 acres are actually deeded. Crown grazing leases, federal lands administered by the province of British Columbia in the residents' interests, comprise the remaining 736,000 acres.

Larry Ramstad and his crew have had more than enough time to retake the Gang Ranch and build the cattle herd into a productive, cohesive commercial unit. Old-timers always have said it takes 10 years to turn things around and create a herd of mature cows, bulls and young females worthy of a cattleman's pride.

"We're a one-iron outfit," Ramstad stated, "and we offer high-quality black cattle. The steers are knife-cut (buyer confidence is assured if the steers look like steers), and all the sale calves, both steers and heifers, are age-certified and preconditioned, and they have not had any implants."

Such a well-defined management strategy reflects the current owner's simple requirement that the ranch hold its own economically. About 600 heifers are bred annually, with 500 or so being kept as replacements. Heifers calve in late February near the headquarters, and are then turned onto dry spring grass, as are the cows that calve in mid-March. Branding, which lasts about three weeks, begins in early June.

The main herd of about 2,500 cows is moved in smaller groups of roughly 400 head to new pasture every three weeks. Following a grazing flow chart set up by the forestry service and ranch manager, cows work their way across mid-elevation grasslands toward the backcountry of Fosberry Meadows and Hungry Valley, even as far as Graveyard Valley. Calves are weaned in

The hardy souls who inhabit the Gang would not trade such views for any that civilization has to offer.

The mountain ranges that almost seem to protect those within their perimeter suck moisture from Pacific storm clouds long before they reach the ranch.

the fall, when cows are pregnancy-checked, vaccinated and turned out to graze. About Christmas, feeding begins and usually lasts through April.

Surprisingly, the Gang can enjoy mild winters, and the feed grounds are in an arid, protected valley. Despite temperatures that hover at about 5 degrees, consistently cold weather is best because fluctuating temperatures lead to thaws, freezes and muddy feed grounds, none conducive to bovine health.

Cattle thrive on the ranch and respect the cowboys, as well. Professional cowhands and buckaroos understand that effective cattle-handling is not a fear-based activity, but a relationship between cowboy, horse and cow. This is more of an understanding that requires patience, an open mind and, above all, a sense of humor, especially on the Chilcotin side of the river.

Simply put, ranching this far from civilization means the cowboys learn to roll with the punches. Far too many things over which they have no control can occur. So cowboys supplement their frustration with humor, even though it can be dark humor; otherwise, they would succumb to the stress.

The Convoluted Horse Program

The Gang Ranch horse program can best be described as convoluted, with no actual breeding direction having been set in stone during the ranch's century and a half of existence. Just as well, some say, because the Gang's freeze-branded ranch horses have never been influenced by those who judge

a horse's merit in the arena. Here, in the Chilcotin, the grand arena has quicksand at one end, thick timber at the other, and a thousand miles in between. A No. 2 shoe on the front and feathers all around are considered attributes.

"We had some Blondies Dude and Boston Mac blood in the past," Ramstad related of the ranch's most recent stud battery, "but now it's mostly Hancock."

The 15 to 20 broodmares are rarely power-bred, chosen instead for their ability to produce cowboy horses that can make long circles, handle major changes in elevation, and maintain body condition during rotational rest periods. Fillies are ridden, and the best ones later might be added to the broodmare band. A working remuda of about 80 head serves approximately seven cowboys. Altogether, there are some 140 head on the outfit, including broodmares, yearlings, 2- and 3-year-olds and the remuda, whose members range from 4 to 15 years of age.

More so, perhaps, than on any other ranch in North America, the horses that call this place home must be quintessentially reliable. Anything less could jeopardize a life, which, as much as anything, has to do with the odds of getting in a bind in remote and rough country.

The odds of getting in an average horse wreck are about the same on the Gang as on many ranches, but the odds of getting out of the wreck in good shape are reduced dramatically on this particular outfit. Good luck to the other hands trying to find a hurt cowboy—the country is just that big. Even if a cowboy is found, no ambulance or Life Flight can easily reach him, and often, by the time he has been found, Mother Nature already has tried to finish him with hypothermia or exposure.

The Gang's Final Say

Ever since Thaddeus and Jerome Harper swam the first cows across the Fraser River back in 1865, the remarkable Gang Ranch has overcome almost impossible odds in its fight for survival as one of North America's largest working cow outfits. In stark contrast to famous, well-managed family ranches established during the same time period, the Gang often was treated like a stray dog, offered a bone when someone felt sympathetic and abused at will, but never really afforded the quality care and attention it deserved. Even major portions of the original holdings have been sold through the years. But the single largest piece of ground, the one that appeals most to those looking for the supreme cowboy adventure, remains intact on the shores of the mysterious Chilcotin.

Today devastating insect infestation has killed the forests that covered the country in a protective blanket. Square miles of trees affected by the pine-bark beetle turn tinderbox dry and reddish-brown, setting up the entire area for a massive cleansing fire, an event that historically occurred every 15 years or so until the white man arrived. But rejuvenation still can occur in this harsh environment, and ranchers sometimes have witnessed miracles.

"The bunchgrass is starting to come back," Ramstad said quietly while kneeling in the dust. He closely inspected a high-traffic pasture area that had been decimated by overgrazing decades before he ever bought his first saddle.

To a cowboy, the term "bunchgrass" actually refers to bluebunch wheatgrass, a delicate plant that funnels rainwater from its outstretched shoots into the main root ball at the plant's center. To drive over the bunchgrass with a vehicle is akin to stealing horses in the Old West. Tires kill the plants, and the tracks remain for years to tell the tale.

Maybe the bunchgrass was never really capable of disappearing for good, much like

Gang Ranch Timeline

1854: Thaddeus and Jerome Harper left San Francisco headed for the gold fields in the colony of British Columbia. But rather than dig for gold, they built a sawmill and bought cattle and land.

1864: The brothers first saw the Chilcotin grasslands across the Fraser River. Adding to their already impressive holding of grazing lands, Thaddeus obtained a Crown grant to 160 acres of creek bottom known as Home Ranch Valley, which became the nucleus of today's Gang Ranch.

1884: Thaddeus Harper registered the J-connected-H brand by combining the initials in his brother's name.

1885: Thaddeus Harper partnered with English publisher Thomas Galpin to create Western Canadian Ranching Company Ltd. Now the largest ranch in Canada, the "Gang," as it came to be known, controlled more than 4 million acres of deeded and federal grazing allotments at its peak in the 1930s.

1912: Construction was completed on the suspension bridge spanning the Fraser River below the ranch headquarters. The bridge, in use to this day, remains the primary access between the ranch and civilization.

1947: Western Canadian Ranching Company Ltd. sold the Gang Ranch to American cattlemen Patrick Studdert and Floyd Skelton. Property sell-offs began at this point, and the original ranch holdings were cut drastically.

1978: The ranch sold to Dale Alsager, a Canadian businessman who involved his family in ownership and management responsibilities. More sell-offs continued, reducing the ranch to its current size of 770,000 acres.

1982: The Alsagers failed to hold onto the operation, declaring bankruptcy in their fourth year. The Gang sold once more, this time to a consortium of several Canadian cattlemen and Ibrahim Afandi, a Saudi Arabian member of BSA Investments Ltd.

1987: After five years of turmoil trying to recreate the Gang Ranch as a tourist destination, rather than a working cattle ranch, BSA Investments Ltd. bought out the Canadian partners, and Ibrahim Afandi became the principal owner.

1989: Larry Ramstad took over as ranch manager. Afandi's hold-steady approach, coupled with Ramstad's keen understanding of ranching in the unforgiving Chilcotin, positioned the Gang Ranch on a path toward healing.

1990 – Present: Following decades of neglect and abuse during the ranch's tumultuous history of absentee ownership and mismanagement, the Gang Ranch finally has regained its place of respect among the largest, productive, rough-country cattle ranches in North America.

the strong, hardy people who keep returning to this strangely attractive, often unforgiving place. To those who call these quiet, windswept grasslands home, the Gang Ranch embodies the very spirits of the cow, the bear, the cowboy and the Chilcotin. None of these wild things can be forced to do what they cannot, or will not, do. The ranch has a certain earthly power, it seems, over everything that lives on it. In the end, it always has the final say.

AUTHORS' PROFILES

Holly Endersby

As a Midwestern city kid, Holly Endersby longed to spend time outdoors, especially with horses. She moved to Oregon to do graduate work and has spent all her adult life in the West. After a 15-year stint as a school principal, she retired early to spend even more time in the outdoors as a freelance writer.

Since then, Holly explained, "It's been my privilege to travel the backcountry with my husband, Scott Stouder, and our pack string—hunting, fishing and riding as I gather material for articles along the way. Assignments have taken me to places many people can only dream about. From rafting remote Arctic rivers to fly-fishing blue-ribbon streams to snowshoeing through fresh powder in the wilderness, my life has been a series of adventures.

"And, as a bonus, the assignments that have led me to these special places also have introduced me to a host of wonderful folks along the way, including those in this book. Horses, wild country and people connected to the land always will hold a special place in my heart."

Guy de Galard

Since childhood, Guy de Galard has had a passion for horses and the American West. Born in Paris, France, Guy began riding at age 6, when a friend's father, who owned an equestrian center, put Guy atop a pony for a short ride. By the time he was 8, Guy rode horseback on a regular basis and went on to jumping and cross-country riding by age 12.

He first heard about Wyoming at age 10, while reading *My Friend Flicka*. He soon became a devoted fan of western movies and television series, living the cowboy lifestyle vicariously through the fictional characters and their French-dubbed horseback adventures.

A self-taught photographer, Guy first took up the craft while attending business school in Paris. As a writer and photographer, he is drawn to authenticity and tradition. His photos, typically rich in color and light, convey action, horsemanship and the rituals of the West. Guy looks for the kind of images that made him dream as a kid and for those that still make him dream today.

After his move to the United States 22 years ago, Guy began to portray what naturally inspired him the most—horses and cowboys. When Guy and his wife, Kristin, relocated from California to the cowboy state of Wyoming seven years ago, he fulfilled his dream to primarily photograph and write about horses and cowboys.

"We longed for wide-open spaces and I wanted more opportunities for western photography and stories about the West," Guy explained. "Being able to ride has helped me a lot in my job. When I am on an assignment at a ranch and saddle up in the morning with the cowboys, I am not just a reporter—I become part of the crew for that day."

Kathy McCraine

Kathy McCraine has been involved with ranching and writing about it most of her life. Born in Texas, she grew up on a ranch in Arizona and graduated from the University of Arizona with a B.A. degree in journalism and a minor in art. After college she worked for and/or edited several livestock publications, including *Western Livestock Journal, Record Stockman,* and *Brangus Journal.*

In 1978 she founded Livestock Communications, one of the first advertising agencies to specialize in livestock. In the mid-1980s she returned to Arizona, where she continued that business and also edited the *Arizona Cattlelog* and *Arizona Quarter Horse* magazines.

From 1993-'95 she published the *Arizona Rancher* magazine, a bi-monthly devoted to the Arizona cattle and horse industries. She also published, wrote and illustrated three cookbooks. Most recently she helped edit and illustrate *Keepers of the Range,* the 100-year history of the Arizona Cattle Growers' Association. Through the years, Kathy, a member of the Livestock Publications Council, has won numerous awards for both feature writing and advertising.

Today Kathy and her husband, Swayze, own Camp Wood Cattle Company near Prescott, Ariz., where they run about 600 commercial cows and raise registered Quarter Horses. She also continues her work as a freelance writer and photographer, with a goal of documenting and preserving the heritage of American ranching.

Tim O'Byrne

Tim O'Byrne was born in Zweibrucken, Germany, the son of a career Air Force man stationed overseas. His father retired in Calgary, Alberta, in 1975, and after graduating high school two years later, Tim took up cowboying. The following 17 years he rode for large-scale commercial cattle ranches in Nevada, Alberta and British Columbia, eventually holding positions as Chapperon foreman at Douglas Lake Ranch and cowboss of the Gang Ranch. To round out his experience in the feedlot, he spent time as Homelot foreman at Van Raay Farms in Alberta, an 85,000-head cattle feeding operation.

O'Byrne and his wife, Christine, launched Calico Beef Consulting in 1994. Their consulting business focuses on cattle handling, facility design, livestock transportation, animal welfare policy and agricultural law.

Tim has been published more than 150 times in such magazines as *Western Horseman* and *Canadian Cattleman* and has authored two books on the lifestyle of working cowboys. *Western Horseman's* book division publishes his latest book, the award-winning *Cowboys and Buckaroos, Trade Secrets of a North American Icon.*

O'Byrne is the editor of *Working Ranch* magazine. He and Christine live in Henderson, Nev., and their son, Mark, is a United States Marine.